GW00362396

The End of Shops

For retailers it is a struggle of line:
adapt to customer behaviour of close the shop

The End of Shops

Social Buying and the Battle for the Customer

COR MOLENAAR

GOWER

© Cor Molenaar 2013

All rights reserved. No part of this publication may be reproduced, stored in a retrieval system or transmitted in any form or by any means, electronic, mechanical, photocopying, recording or otherwise without the prior permission of the publisher.

Cor Molenaar has asserted his moral right under the Copyright, Designs and Patents Act, 1988, to be identified as the author of this work.

Published by
Gower Publishing Limited
Wey Court East
Union Road
Farnham
Surrey, GU9 7PT
England

Ashgate Publishing Company
110 Cherry Street
Suite 3-1
Burlington, VT 05401-3818
USA

www.gowerpublishing.com

British Library Cataloguing in Publication Data
Molenaar, Cor.
  The end of shops : social buying and the battle for the customer.
  1. Consumer behavior. 2. Teleshopping. 3. Retail trade.
  4. Retail trade--Technological innovations.
  I. Title
  658.8'7-dc23

Library of Congress Cataloging-in-Publication Data
Molenaar, Cor.
  The end of shops : social buying and the battle for the customer / by Cor Molenaar.
      p. cm.
  Includes bibliographical references and index.
  ISBN 978-1-4094-4974-4 (hbk) -- ISBN 978-1-4094-4975-1 (ebk) 1. Electronic commerce.
  2. Internet marketing. 3. Teleshopping. 4. Retail trade. 5. Consumer behavior. I. Title.
  HF5548.32.M647 2013
  658.8'72--dc23

                                                                                2012035591

ISBN 978 1 4094 4974 4 (hbk)
ISBN 978 1 4094 4975 1 (ebk – PDF)
ISBN 978 1 4094 6502 7 (ebk – ePUB)

MIX
Paper from
responsible sources
FSC® C018575

Printed and bound in Great Britain
by MPG PRINTGROUP

Contents

List of Figures and Tables

Figures

Tables

About the Author

Professor Cor Molenaar is Professor by Special Appointment of e-Marketing and Distance Selling at RSM/Erasmus University in Rotterdam. He is also the chairman of the *Stichting Certificering Thuiswinkelwaarborg* (Home Shopping Guarantee Hallmark) and chairman of the RFID platform in the Netherlands. He is also involved with the NIMA, the Dutch Institute for Marketing, as a member of the Examination Board charged with (among other things) the e-marketing of exams.

He is director of the strategic advice bureau eXQuo Consultancy in Oosterbeek, the Netherlands. In this function he advises and supports businesses of various sizes from different markets such as financial institutes, manufacturers, retail organisations and service companies. He also organises workshops, boardroom sessions and in-company training sessions. He gives many lectures, both at home and abroad.

He is the author of a number of books. Prior to the book *The End of Shops* he published *eStrategy* (2000) and *Shopping 3.0* (2010). For higher education and university students he also wrote the textbook *eMarketing* (2010).

The chair in e-Marketing and Distance Selling at the RSM/Erasmus University has been made possible by Cap Gemini, Hybris Software, GFK marktonderzoek and Thuiswinkel.Org (sub sponsors: Achmea, Bol.nl, Conrad electronics, ECI, Sundio/Sunweb, Wehkamp.nl). More information about Cor Molenaar can be found at the following websites:

www.cormolenaar.nl

www.eindevandewinkel.nl

THE BATTLE OF THE SHOP:
FIGHTING AT VARIOUS FRONTS TO SURVIVE!

A shop has to fight at various fronts to survive, and that is no easy task. In this book I will take a comprehensive look at this: the battle, the dangers and the opportunities. A theatre of war with many losers, but also winners.

The Theatre of War, the Danger

The Internet is a major threat as there is suddenly competition from unknown suppliers and from suppliers who have fewer restrictions such as opening hours or physical location.

Suppliers who also sell on the Internet. Brand manufacturers sell via their own sites and have their own e-marketing strategy, in which they can invest more money than most retailers. Whether this also leads to more sales for the existing shops, however, is the question. Brand manufacturers also want to open their own shops, the so-called 'experience shops', or Flag stores, maintain their own customer database, send newsletters and have their own webshop.

Customers have a new buying behaviour in which the Internet is integrated. No-nonsense products, such as foodstuffs and household goods are still bought locally, with emotional products also being bought on impulse. The more well-considered purchases, however, are increasingly being carried out on the Internet. As a result, the market for physical products such as books, music and women's clothes, is decreasing. What's more, the large webshops on the Internet are becoming increasingly often total suppliers, resulting in them looking more like the physical shops (see e.g. Amazon.com).

New buying behaviour leads to a decomposition of the buying process. Information becomes detached from buying. Initially this took place in the travel sector, whereby the customer can now put together his own package: travel, hotel and hire a car. These are three different types of bookings, which are now conveniently grouped together on sites such as those of Transavia and Ryanair. This detachment from concept to product now occurs more frequently thanks to the Internet. People are basing their searches less on shops and increasingly on products. The order of the choices made was always first a shop and then the product. This is why the location and product range was so important in the retail trade. Trust was placed in the shop. Now increasingly people will first choose a product, and then look for a suitable shop. As a result the bond with the product (brand) and consequently the power of the manufacturer is growing.

The Change

These days customers buy in a different way than they did before. They first look on the Internet for what they want to buy, look at the prices, compare the products and only then do they decide where to buy it. Buying in a shop has now become an option; it is no longer a necessity. This new buying behaviour, 'the new shopping ', has to be a guiding principle for the retail trade.

Introduction

The book *Shopping 3.0* describes how the buying behaviour of customers is changing radically. This can be a threat to retailers, but if they adapt to these changes then this can also lead to opportunities. In this book I wish to examine these threats to retailers as well as to outline the opportunities. For retailers who cannot, or do not wish to, change 'the end of the shops' is a given. In order to survive they have to change, otherwise they will not fit into the new retailer landscape that is a consequence of the new shopping. It starts with looking at and listening to customers. They are unwittingly determining the future.

As part of the development of this book, studies were carried out by e-Marketing and Distance Selling students at the RSM/Erasmus University. I have also talked with entrepreneurs about their ideas regarding the future, and looked at practical examples to illustrate the changes which are taking place. I present the views and examples towards the back of this book.

Structure of the Book

After the introductory Chapter 1, Chapter 2 examines customer behaviour: what does the customer want and how do they buy? What changes can be expected? Chapter 3 looks at the retail trade: one's own shop, how it used to be, how it is and what it has to become. Is there a future for the shop? A webshop is often regarded as the solution, but is that really the case? This will be examined in Chapter 4: is the Internet the new high street or will it not go as far as all that? On the basis of this question, Chapter 5 will examine the changes and solutions. What are the new developments that are being facilitated by technological applications, and what opportunities do they offer for shops? Chapter 6 analyses new business models. Do these provide shops with a future? Deciding which of these business models will be successful is rather difficult! Finally, experts and entrepreneurs are asked how they view these changes and what opportunities they see in the future combined with some practical developments. Even though their views come from various perspectives, they are unanimous in their conclusion: a great deal is going to change, as a result of changes brought about by different customer behaviour, the new shopping, as well as by different retail concepts that are supported with the latest technology. The opportunities provided by the Internet and the consequences of the developments for one's own business model are a challenge for every retailer.

The customer can choose where to shop, and therefore also needs to be motivated to buy. This book provides an overview of the developments in buying behaviour, the changes in what's actually being sold, and the opportunities for the physical retail. In addition, I will also keep you up to date via Twitter, my website www.cormolenaar.nl and through my newsletters.

Professor Dr C.N.A. Molenaar
Oosterbeek
cor@cormolenaar.nl

1

The End of Shops? Why It Is No Longer Necessary to Go to a Shop!

Introduction

The buying behaviour of customers has changed over the last few years. Not only has the Internet played a major role, but so too have the increased mobility and freedom of choice. The book *Shopping 3.0* (2009) took a detailed look at this change in buying behaviour, whereby the role of the Internet has been particularly important. Picking up ordered items from the shops, via click and collect was already particularly popular in England, whereas we are only now beginning to see this emerge on the European continent. The coined phrase *click and collect* has now become well-known, thanks to the department store John Lewis. Another department store, Debenhams, then quickly came up with the phrase *buy and collect* for the same service. An important role of the Internet is the possibility it provides for orientation and acquiring information before deciding to buy. Based on this principle the idea rose that real shops also need a webshop; the real shop will be an important collecting point for customers. The future of retailing might be the integration of Internet and bricks, as we can see later on.

Out-of-town shopping centres have become very popular in England. They have led to changes in the products offered in shops in the traditional city centres, and partly, as a consequence of this, to a reduction of the buying public in cities. City centres in England have changed rapidly over the first decade of the twenty-first century. We are now seeing similar developments in other countries in Europe.

As indicated in the book *Shopping 3.0*, the Internet era only really began in 2008. Prior to that there was Internet, but it did not form an integral part of people's behaviour. We saw this change in 2008, and this is becoming increasingly clear. Tablet computers, iPads and smartphones are all signs of this change. Cloud computing is already possible and will facilitate this change even further. People will always be *connected* and identifiable, wherever they are, particularly in shops.

Although the book *Shopping 3.0* analysed the change in behaviour from the customer's perspective, it did not examine the possibilities and changes for retail. This book, *The End of Shops*, therefore takes a closer look at the changes that are the consequence of the new buying behaviour from the perspective of the retailer. The changes in the buying behaviour, the possibilities of technology and the opportunities and problems of webshops are all given close scrutiny. These changes can be a threat to the existing retail trade. Sometimes Shopping 3.0, whereby customers use both the Internet and physical shops in a buying process, is seen as Retailing 3.0. This is, however, a misconception, as this would mean that the future of the existing retail lies also in the Internet. This is incorrect as shopping is aimed at the buying behaviour and the degree to which the Internet forms part of the buying process. In contrast, retailing is part of selling and the degree to which the Internet forms part of the selling process and the degree to which the focus is on the individual customer: from selling paradigm to buying paradigm. Previously, people had to go to shops to buy; now they *can* go to shops, but they can also visit webshops, or both, as part of a buying process.

There is a clear development in the buying behaviour, from buying in the shop to a combination of shop and other possibilities such as the Internet. There is also a development in retailing from a focus on sales (sales paradigm) to a focus on the needs of the customer (demand paradigm).

Table 1.1   Difference between shopping and retailing

Buying	Characterisation	Selling	Characterisation
Shopping 1.0	Traditional shopping from a stall, shop or artisan.	Retailing 1.0	Traditional supply via a physical location, personal contact with customers. **Sales paradigm**
Shopping 2.0	Non-store buying via mail order, coupon or the Internet.	Retailing 2.0	Non-physical selling via mail order, coupon or the Internet. No personal contact with customers. **Sales paradigm**
Shopping 3.0	Cross-retailing, buying process via various channels. Orientation and getting information usually takes place on the Internet, with the buying taking place in the shop or also on the Internet.	Retailing 3.0	Customer central, **buying paradigm**. Both physical and non-physical, both standard products and customised products.

The future for physical retail actually lies in this supply chain reversal, where the customer is central. This means that retailers must adapt all processes, business models and products on offer to the wishes and behaviour of the customers. What's more, it is important to open shops in areas where you expect to find customers. There is, of course, a difference in the buying behaviour we see in shopping and when doing the groceries.[1] When doing the groceries, speed and convenience are often important, usually one-stop-shopping for greater efficiency. Shopping, on the other hand, is looking, searching and buying. It is those big changes in customers' buying behaviour that we see in this type of shopping. Retailers must be aware that customers have a choice of whether to shop and where to do it, and that customers often also enjoy shopping. Shopping has therefore become a form of recreation, and shops should therefore be interesting, fun and welcoming. This requires a new view on retail, new business models, and new forms of partnership with suppliers as well as with customers. It is these possibilities and opportunities for the physical retail as a result of this new shopping behaviour that will be examined in this book. There are still many possibilities for a promising future, but one has to be willing to change in a way that is appealing to the customer, otherwise a place in a museum is the most one can expect. Shoppers should be encouraged to shop, not punished for their shopping behaviour. Motivate people to go to your shop or go to town to shop; do not punish them for entering a shop.

The Behaviour of the Modern Consumer?

A retail landscape is emerging, the contours of which are slowly becoming apparent. We are seeing more and more empty shops along shopping streets, and shop premises being taken over by restaurants, snack bars and cafes. What's more, retailers are being discouraged by the high rents, the inaccessibility for cars, the high parking costs as well as the bad weather. Also, the empty shops in the high street are not adding to the shopping pleasure. Shopping streets are becoming unwelcoming and depressing, whilst the shops themselves and the sales staff often do not help the situation much.

> *Do not touch. Exchange is not possible. No, we cannot order. We do not deliver the product to your door, or perhaps next week on Wednesday but we don't know what time.*

---

[1] See, for example, the interview with entrepreneurs at ISMinstituut: http://ism instituut.nl/archives/436

The modern consumer wants convenience, service and to be treated as a customer when he or she is out shopping – in the mornings, afternoons and evenings, always accessible, *always connected*. This modern consumer lives in different way than those of previous generation(s), has other demands, other priorities and, above all, is in a hurry! This generation is very time-conscious, is critical about the conditions and is hard to please. Can shops still meet these demands?

Shops have restricted opening hours, approximately 54 hours per week out of a total of 168 hours, which is just 33% of the potential buying time. Late-night shopping and Sunday shopping, as well as the standard opening hours, are also restricted in many countries in Europe. When the shops are open on a Sunday they tend to heave with customers. Late-night shopping is often more pleasant than daytime shopping, but the opening hours are not adjusted according to the buying wishes, but rather to the wishes of the policymakers. Even supermarkets are increasingly arguing for being able to open on Sundays. The opening hours and the shops have to be in line with the wishes of the politicians who formulate regulations from another perspective than that of the retailers and certainly from a different perspective than that of the customer. But will it stay this way? Experiences with Sunday shopping and late-night shopping are very positive. In England and certainly in America we see people making well-considered purchases and going to shops at times that suit them. Apple stores sometimes do not shut at all, but stay open day and night and yet always seem to be busy! The ultimate shopping experience.

People seem to be happier on Sundays, so the buying resistance is low. We want to treat ourselves. On Mondays, in contrast, we tend to be a little down, so there tends to be the highest shopping resistance then. So why are the shops closed on Sundays when we feel happy and yet open on Mondays when we do not feel our best? Buying is *fun*. It has become a recreational activity, no longer a necessity. Why shouldn't you be able to recreate when and where you want to? A conflict between legislators, retailers and customers is becoming apparent. But despite great pressure and a considerably restrictive policy, other roads suddenly appear to be possible.

People go en masse to car boot sales, to fetes in villages and cities as well as to outlet centres and out-of-town shopping centres. Customers look for shopping centres that are open when they feel like having a day out, for example at IKEA where the kids can enjoy the play area and the family can treat themselves to Swedish meatballs. Heavily laden shopping trolleys, filled with goods all impulsively bought, show that shopping is *fun*. And we are really active on the Internet through Google, Facebook, Twitter and other social media. We are looking, finding, communicating and being social. We want to show our communicative side, without inhibitions and without anxieties. The Internet has become an important means for recreation, a means of communication for looking up others, often strangers, and often sharing our most intimate feelings. *Social media, social buying* and *social shopping* are forms of *social individualism* with which we feel comfortable, but within a world surrounded by friends, acquaintances and strangers. We feel happy because we can finally do what we have always dreamt of: meeting one another when *we* want to, shopping when *we* feel like it; gaming, going on dates and relaxing, with friends and strangers, simply because we happen to feel like it. Time, place and circumstances do not matter as long as we are happy. Do shops still fit into this picture?

Shops or Products?

Shopping has become a form of recreation and no longer a 'necessary evil'. You can choose where and when you shop: we buy our essential items from nearby shops and the other products we buy where it suits us. Do we use the Internet for convenience or through impatience? Also, the very foundation of shopping is under discussion; why does the customer actually buy in a shop? Is it because of the shop itself or because of the products? Increasingly, customers first choose a product (branded article) and then look for a shop to buy it in (a physical shop or a webshop). This results in the declining appeal of shops but the increasing appeal of the product. These days customers are more easily inclined to change shops and to switch more often between the Internet and shops. A different kind of playing field has arisen where existing shops have to re-evaluate the distinctive benefits they offer. This in turn has also led to competition with (brand) manufacturers. Manufacturers now also have opportunities to develop a direct relationship with the final customer and communicate directly with them. It is therefore logical to sell the product directly to the final customer, through the Internet or one's own shop. This then becomes a battle for the loyalty or brand preference of the customer. If a customer has a strong brand preference then the product tends to be bought from the manufacturer. However, if a customer wants to have some choice, and perhaps also advice, then he will tend to buy in a shop (physical or webshop). And this is where the strength of the retail trade lies, but then of course this strength would have to be used. This can be done by providing independent advice, putting across a feeling of trust and developing loyalty. Customers can choose where they buy: from the shop, from the manufacturer, on the Internet, but also from abroad, from the market or even from a private individual on eBay. There is plenty of choice.

The Shop has to Change

Not so long ago you would automatically go to a shop to buy a product or just to look around. That is not the case these days. There is now a choice between webshops and physical shops, between the flagship stores of manufacturers and the standard shops in the shopping street, between local shops and shops further away in a shopping centre. Shops have to prove themselves once more and rediscover themselves. They have to work out again what is their unique benefit for the customer. In order to achieve this, the retailer has to look closely into the *why* question: why do customers buy from a shop? Now and again a shopkeeper should stand outside his own shop and look at how the customers walk, browse and choose in their shop. Compare your shop with both successful and less successful competitors, and assess what is good as well as bad about your own shop. Have a look abroad, and be open-minded. After all, this is what the customer is.

Take a look at the Internet, buy something, look at the delivery conditions and compare these with your own shop. Physical shops have many disadvantages, physical disadvantages: accessibility, opening hours and a high level of fixed costs. The customer experiences these disadvantages as well, so a shop should compensate these with the advantages that only a shop can provide: the local presence, the personal contact, the product range, the choice on offer. The shop must prove itself once more to its customers. In doing so, the shopkeeper should not only look at the old way of retailing, such as effective purchasing, a suitable location and an appropriate product range, but also integrate modern possibilities.

Examples include Internet in the shop, and perhaps also the shop on the Internet. One also needs to look not only at rational aspects but also at emotional aspects, and not only at services but also at hospitality. The customer has choices. The customer therefore has to be motivated and services offered. The customer above all has to feel welcome. Consider, for example, a social corner with newspapers, magazines and coffee, surrounded by smiling and friendly personnel – videos and music in the shop, attractive posters and terminals where purchases can be made. It is not so difficult, but the step *from selling to buying* is a major change for the retailer. This, however, is the change that will determine whether the shop will still be around in 10 years' time.

Attention also has to be given to the new business concepts, which have to be not product-based but purchase-based. What's more, retailers have to look at new business models and examine why everything is transaction-based and not customer-based. Traditionally the shop was the last link in a *supply chain*, but why is the shop not the first link in a *buying chain* or a *buying concept*? Models that are now successful on the Internet can also provide the leitmotiv in the real world (see Chapter 6).

The Challenge for the Future

Another way of thinking is essential, a way that starts with customers and that requires collaboration between suppliers and retailers. Only if this happens and only if suppliers and retailers both want to collaborate in a change to the shop, in terms of look and feel, opening hours, concepts and the financial model, will there be a future for shops. The old approach by contrast simply focused on the property and profit per transaction. These matters had very little to do with customers. Due to the Internet and the greater freedom of choice enjoyed by customers, the margins are being placed under a great deal of pressure. In addition, due to the new buying behaviour it is no longer necessary to go to a shop. Increased numbers of empty properties and a smaller buying public means a reduction in the value of property.

The retail sector has to reflect upon the situation and assess once more whether they have a future and how to make this future profitable. If this does not happen, the future of shops will lie on the Internet and in large shopping centres. This will mean the end of the pleasant small shops in villages, neighbourhoods and cities. Customers buy differently, the business itself is not sufficient for the new challenge of the future, and what's more a business model based on transaction profits is also something of the past. Times have changed and the way business is done has to change accordingly. In countries such as England you see city centres changing as the larger shops move elsewhere, but we can see a similar pattern in the Netherlands, Belgium, France and Germany. Starbucks, smaller cafes, restaurants and bars are beginning to flourish in city centres, as well as small pleasant shops that are suddenly grabbing hold of their opportunity.

> *When in a forest the large trees are felled, the sun and rain can once again reach the ground, helping to stimulate new life. A variety of plants can grow to form new vegetation and natural beauty. But without the felling of the large trees this would never have been possible. A wise biological lesson for the retailer!*

The future lies with a collaboration of retailers and suppliers, but also collaboration with city councils and real estate owners and retailers and customers, a concept that is based on *social shopping* and *social buying*. Customers, after all, are people who make decisions based on human motives and who respond through human rationality. So it is here where the opportunity lies for the current retail trade. There are certainly new opportunities, but at the same time it will also be curtains for many retailers who hold onto the old principles and habits. The future is not about selling but about buying!

A great deal still has to happen in order to secure the future of shops, at governmental level and local level, with the shopkeepers, city planners and project developers. If there is no collaboration then the future will be rather bleak. The end of shops is approaching. Fortunately, it's the eleventh hour of shops in general; however, that does not mean that for many shops it is already too late. The old business model based on the value of property, *bonuses of suppliers* and transaction profits has had its day. In order to survive a new strategy and new business model are necessary. But then, if customers no longer come to you to buy, you are no longer meeting a need and isn't that, after all, what retailing is *also* about?

Conclusion and Summary of Chapter 1

There is a difference between the traditional retail whereby location and product range were important and there was a strong focus on transactions, and the new retail where it is the customers' needs and wishes that are central.

Table 1.2   **Summary of Chapter 1, the difference between traditional retail and new opportunities**

Retail	Traditional	New
Product range in the shop.	City centres and in shopping centres, shopping streets.	High-profile location A1, out-of-town centres and small shops in centres and cities.
Buying behaviour.	Everything in the shop.	Orientating and acquiring information on the Internet, choice of buying in the shop or on the Internet.
Value driver.	Available at the right location, the right product range.	Service, advice, trust and seeing /taking articles.
Money maker.	Transaction profits, trade margin.	Other elements, service modules, customer value, relationships/affiliates.
Focus.	Sales, realising transactions .	Demand, building relationships.

2

The New Buying Behaviour:
The Consumer of Today

You can't fool us, we know everything and are highly critical.

The new shopping behaviour reveals that we really do buy differently from how we did roughly a decade ago. Shopping has become very easy, sitting comfortably on the sofa, in front of the television with the laptop or iPad on your lap. By having Wi-Fi in the living room, the computer user is no longer confined to an isolated corner of the house. Going on the web has now become part of the evening's recreation. On Twitter, Facebook, just surfing or simply shopping whilst on the sofa, we do it every evening and often also during the day. We still enjoy going to the shops to see and feel the products, and to take them home with us. But will it always be like this once Internet reaches adulthood?

Surfing on the Sofa

These days the Internet is an integral part of our lives. Not being able to go onto the Internet sometimes even leads to stressful situations, certainly to frustration – for the user, that is. Of course, the Internet is much more than just shopping: buying on the Internet accounts for only 7% of the use of this medium. The average person also enjoys gaming, looking at video clips or simply surfing or chatting on social media sites. These activities are much more important than shopping. As a result, Internet use has become at least as important as watching television. And it is not really a choice, as the two go well together. Watching television while having your laptop or iPad within reach is becoming increasingly popular. People want to be accessible and to give their opinions. Being isolated at home, in your own cocoon, is a thing of the past. Via Twitter you give your opinion on television programmes and respond to one another. Interactive television is now possible, but in a different way from how we had imagined it. Responding directly to the programme using email, chat and Twitter is fun, but talking to one another online and complaining about a television programme is even more enjoyable. It is quite striking to see the different ways in which people complain and to see the humour they use. Following the comments on Twitter can be even more entertaining than watching the programme itself. The Internet is becoming increasingly integrated within our everyday behaviour. Many European countries show a similar behaviour towards the Internet.

Internet enables you to respond to all sorts of things, which in turn also elicits responses from other people. Blogging, micro-blogging (Twitter) or social media such as Facebook allow us to chat with one another. The Internet makes the world suddenly very transparent and accessible. Whatever it is you are looking for, the relevant website is only a click away. There are actually no secrets anymore and there is certainly no longer any privacy. The information function has become a very important aspect of the Internet and this easy accessibility of information has been a major factor in our changing behaviour. We have become wiser and well informed about what is available, wherever it may be.

The possibilities of finding information about products, companies or people through the Internet are practically endless. We want to, and are able to, know everything and communicate about all sorts of things. This has a direct effect on our actual behaviour, both in private and professionally. Boundaries become faded as a consequence. This also applies to the differences between the products offered by shops and between webshops and physical shops. We can buy 24/7, find everything on the Internet and buy when and where it suits us, while the existing physical shops still have limited opening hours, a limited product range and, of course, also a limited reach. The challenge for shops is clear.

A Different Buying Behaviour

This use of the Internet and the changes in behaviour related to this of course lead to a different sort of buying behaviour at the local shops. Why would you go to a shop when you can buy on your laptop in the comfort of your own home? The items are even delivered to your door. People will certainly continue buying, but will it be in shops? So this is the challenge for shops:

to motivate the customers to buy from you. This motivation never used to be so important. It was a matter of the right location and the right product range. Shops chose a good location, with plenty of passers-by, often near other shops, a little further away from the competition (or intentionally close by) and customers simply came. However, that has now changed thanks to the Internet, as well as to the increased mobility that comes with the increased leisure time. A fine challenge for the shopkeeper, but has this now sealed the fate of the retailer?

The Future of the Retailer

The retailer will only have a future if he takes into account the new buying behaviour and is willing to accept the consequences. The retailer has to change. He may even have to reinvent himself and discover what values or benefits he can offer the customer. The retailer can no longer passively wait for customers, but has to actively attract them. He should no longer focus on selling products, but concentrate more on building and maintaining relationships. The shop attracted customers through its collection and look and feel, but also through the professionalism and personality of the staff. This appeal was reinforced by the close proximity of other shops. Shopping centres had to have at least branches of the major supermarkets and major chain stores that sell clothing and household goods. For this reason shops sought one another out, in city centres, shopping streets and shopping centres. Be close to one another and the customer will surely come was the idea. However, these days customers are not so easily attracted in this manner; and why should they go to a shop when they can buy everything at home? This was recognised (too) late by shopkeepers and is even now still played down. A good analysis of the current behaviour of the shopkeeper and the new behaviour of customers shows that the future is not going to be simply a continuation of the past. Due to the customers' different buying behaviour, the local shopkeeper suddenly has to compete with shops, regardless of where they are located, that have set up a webshop or that are pure players on the Internet. The modern customer is very well informed and so takes a more critical look at products, shops, prices and services. The retail trade therefore has to respond by adapting to the customers' new buying behaviour. And so it is here that the challenge lies for every shopkeeper, regardless of whether he only has a physical shop or also/only a webshop. This challenge applies to manufacturers as well, because what is the best distribution channel these days?

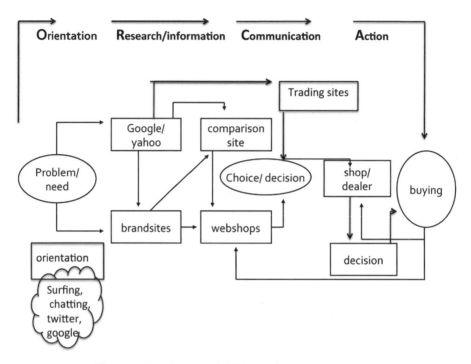

Figure 2.1   The new buying model (ORCA)

FISHERS AND HUNTERS

A fisherman is patient. He carefully picks a spot, a place where he feels comfortable and where the fish bite. He carefully selects his rod, float and weight. Everything necessary to catch the fish is given due consideration; even the net is placed close at hand. His sandwich box and thermos flask with coffee are packed in his bag. The 'long' waiting will start. Just like the typical retailer. The location is chosen with care. The potential customers, the possible turnover and the possible pricing are all examined. The fish are counted and evaluated.

A shop is carefully selected; its size, location, the city and accessibility. The products are chosen, the shop layout determined and shop window display arranged. The float has been chosen and the bait is ready. Now it is a question of waiting for the customer. And at the end of the day the catch is counted. Sometimes another spot is sought or the bait altered. The retailer, too, will sometimes change location, offer discounts or advertise. But the retailer always remains patient and waits for the customer to bite.

But hunting is a different matter altogether! Pick out the gun, find the right bullets and then off you go, sometimes hunting for specific animals, such as wild boar, but usually unexpected animals. Always on the lookout you assess the chances of success and grab the moment when it comes. The typical retailer lacks this skill, whereas this is the strength of a web retailer. Where are the customers, how can I motivate them to buy (create traffic) and how do I ensure that they also come back? Whilst the retailer patiently waits for his customers to come, the web retailer continues hunting. Or perhaps the comparison with a fishing trawler is more appropriate? The active trawler fishes the sea empty whilst the waiting fisherman is left behind, disconsolate.

The new shopping as a process, from orientation, via research/information to communication, and finally action (the ORCA buying model). The Internet plays an important role particularly with orientation and information. Going to the physical shop has become an option.

The Buying Process of Customers

The buying behaviour has four components:

1. You realise that you need or want to buy something (awareness).

2. You ask yourself what and where you want to buy (orientation).

3. Of course you look at the distinctive features and the options (research and information).

4. Advice or consultation is often required, with your partner, friend or the salesperson (communication).

5. You decide what you want to buy and where, and then you do it (action).

As a customer you suddenly become aware that you need something. This will often be a latent desire, which has become a current one. A washing machine breaks down, someone talks about a product, you are hungry or you see, for example, an advertisement that strikes a chord with you. It can, of course, be simply a routine activity whereby you are replenishing the basic necessities at home. You see this, for example, with the supermarket, often a weekly visit just before the weekend. A latent need becomes opportune. The following steps in the buying process greatly depend on the time, place, need, product and customer. For food you go directly to a restaurant, a chippy or a shop without giving it much thought. For your groceries you go to the local shops. This is usually a routine activity to replenish your kitchen cupboards. But with other products you need more time before proceeding to a purchase.

Emotional products, which you can take with you straightaway and whereby the price is not a restriction, are bought in the shop or these days also on the Internet: seeing, wanting and buying. However, with other products you may want some time to think about it. It is with these sorts of products, which are given more consideration, that we see a change in the buying behaviour, based on an intrinsic behaviour and therefore on who you are and what you want. This can be related to age, gender, ethnicity or character. Anthropological motives often also play a role in this. In order to be able to make a good choice, you first have a good look at what is available. This used to take place in the shop or on the shopping streets. You would walk past various shop windows, go inside some shops and have a look around. You would often speak to the salesperson, take brochures with you or speak to others regarding the possible choices (word of mouth). Then suddenly you decide; the final discussion follows. You would ask for prices and perhaps make a comparison. And then your choice regarding what you want to buy and where you would do it was made. You would then go to the shop, satisfied with your choice, and buy the product. The result: a happy salesperson and a happy customer! This process that starts with becoming aware and ends with the actual purchase can have a time span from just a fraction of a second or a few minutes to perhaps weeks or even months, such as when buying a house or a car.

Traditional Buying Process

In the traditional buying process the salesperson and the shop play an important role. In the shop you can make comparisons (orientation) and acquire information. You are also helped in making a choice. It is logical that the shop has an important role in shopping. Knowledge, expertise, products and services are all present in one place. Shopkeepers therefore provide a real benefit here: location, knowledge, contact and the product range. This is all well and good, but as soon as customers proceed to buy in a different way the role of the shop changes with it, and this is exactly what is happening in the retail sector. Many customers have acquired a different (buying) behaviour, due to all sorts of external circumstances, such as mobility, ambience or the Internet. In part thanks to the increased mobility people can now shop in places that are not necessarily close to home. This can be seen in, for example, the long queues at IKEA, as well as the popular large shopping and outlet centres such as the Trafford Centre, Highbury and all the out-of-town shopping centres. Potential buyers come from far and wide, as long as there is some parking space, coffee and something to eat, and providing these centres satisfy a particular need. If this is not the case then the Internet provides many advantages, and perhaps it would make sense to switch to the Internet for such purchases. This is the case not only with shops but also with service provision through businesses such as

Social Shopping or Social Buying

In addition to the increased mobility, which has led to people buying not only near their homes but also further afield, the social element of shopping is important. Customers have more free time, which they want to spend doing fun things. We wish one another a good weekend, and ask what we have planned. This has therefore become an important aspect of our leisure time. We feel that we deserve to have some fun after a week of hard work. There are, of course, differences between the various age groups. Older people have come into contact with the Internet later on in life. They have a different, more considered view on life, and have strong and clear-cut opinions based on their experience. Younger people, in contrast, learn things more quickly, are mad about technology, are very social. They are the so-called Generation Y or Einstein Generation. Although the different age groups show a different type of behaviour, interaction can frequently be seen. Young people influence the older generation and the technology provides many new possibilities, such as smart phones and computers with Internet.

AGE INFLUENCES (SHOPPING) BEHAVIOUR

The *sixties generation* (baby boomers born between 1945 and 1955) show a group behaviour based on predefined characteristics, such as gender, social class and background.

   The *seventies generation* (born between 1955 in 1965), however, are referred to as a lost generation. The formation of groups takes place on the basis of social identity. This is a generation that is concerned about the future and the environment, and is part of an increased socialisation of society. This generation has a critical attitude towards those in power. Both the sixties and the seventies generations are not very open to change. They are also very reticent when it comes to adopting the Internet. They tend to stick to old values and habits. They will embrace it only if they see real benefits for themselves, but only then within the traditional buying process and without taking any risks.

With the *eighties generation* (born between 1965 and 1975) we can see a sharply increasing individualism. This was in part inspired by the developments of the nineteen eighties, whereby one's own property and standing up for oneself were elevated as the norm once again. The Internet fits in well within this framework, too. This generation has fully accepted the Internet as a medium, and the smartphone is being embraced as a valuable thing to have. These generations are also called web immigrants: the later generations grew up with Internet and are the web-natives. Their behaviour is really different towards (mobile) technology and Internet.

The *nineties generation* witnessed the technical developments during their teenage years, during the introduction of mobile phones and the Internet. This was the first generation that took full advantage of these developments. Due to the many communication possibilities, from text messages to chat, this has become a highly communicative generation. They form social groups based on interests, are highly socially minded and empathise with one another.

The latest generation was born between 1985 and 1995, the Millennial Generation, also referred to as the *Generation Y* and the *Einstein Generation*. This generation is still young and insecure, but technology is a *fact of life* which they can no longer do without. They are always *connected* and have an opinion about everything. They are, however, still critical and look for a reason for using all this technical gadgetry. It is a generation that due to insecurity wants to take part in and belong to it all. *Social grouping, looking one another up on the Internet and sharing activities online* all typify this generation.

Shopping has become part of what we do in our spare time. Shopping therefore has to be fun; emotional aspects have to be added rather than rational ones. Retailers have to realise that we do not *have* to shop but *want* to shop. In our choice regarding where we go shopping, we are led by all sorts of personal motives: do you go alone, with your partner, friends or with your family? How much time do you have? What mood are you in? How you are going to get there (on foot, by bike, car, bus or train)? You often hear considerations such as: 'Check out the latest film at the cinema,' 'Go for a cup of coffee,' 'Go out to play' (children), 'Difficult to park there, you know' or 'Easy parking, always space,' 'It's a short walk from the train station' and 'Shall we also get a bite to eat?' Particularly, older people like shopping. They have the money and plenty of time available – the perfect combination for shopping. But for all the other generations this is no longer a logical choice anymore. The Internet has a stronger influence on the younger generations and choosing to go to the shops is decreasing in popularity with them. Why go to all that trouble when you can have it delivered to your door the following day? Retailers in particular have to be aware of the different behaviour displayed by these different age groups. Older people do actually want to compare on the Internet, but do their shopping in a physical shop.

Social Shopping

Shopping as a form of leisure time is in fact *social shopping*. You shop because it is fun and because you (often) do it with someone else. With *social shopping* what happens around the actual shopping, the peripheral activities, is much more important than visiting the shops themselves. It is about enjoying your time spent with friends and acquaintances. *Social shopping* is different from *social buying*. With *social shopping* the shopping is secondary, whereas with social buying, that is to say buying something together with someone else, it is all about buying. In the case of *social shopping* things may be bought, but not necessarily. This contrasts with *social buying* where something is always bought, or there is at the very least a strong intention to buy. It is all to do with buying, after all!

TRAFFORD CENTRE: ENTERTAINMENT OR SHOPPING CENTRE?

A decade ago one of the largest shopping centres in Europe, the Trafford Centre, was built outside Manchester, England at a large industrial site. This shopping centre, located alongside transhipment companies, factories such as Kellogg's and the football stadium of Manchester United, each weekend attracts thousands of visitors. It has good accessibility, including by public transport, with plenty of parking and numerous entrances via well-known shops such as Debenhams and John Lewis. Inside there is a large, friendly shopping street with smaller shops (on two levels), marble flooring and palm trees. But it is not this pampering concept that lies at the heart of its great appeal – it is the bars and restaurants along with the entertainment centre.

A large cinema complex with numerous screens, a large bar and restaurant complex built to resemble a ship can accommodate more than one thousand visitors. The indoor road that leads from the shopping centre to this large-scale restaurant is a copy of Bourbon Street in New Orleans, with French balconies and many small bars, cafes and restaurants. There are also various events to attract visitors. The opening hours are long, certainly for the smaller shops. Shopping has become a leisure activity, or you could say leisure now offers the possibility of shopping.

TRAFFORD CENTRE

These concepts and motives to go shopping are frequently confused with one another. Women often go shopping with one another to a pleasant shopping centre or to the city centre, to have something to eat and drink and perhaps to do a bit of 'shop surfing'. Buying is of secondary importance and often just incidental. The peripheral aspects, the (outdoor) cafes and restaurants for example, are much more important than the shops; *social shopping*. On Saturdays you will often see couples, usually heading towards very specific shops where the man will try on clothes, whilst the woman gives advice or makes the decisions. Often people help one another when buying. Mobile telephones, electronic goods and household appliances are the kinds of products where a little bit of advice from a confidant is always welcome (even if it is your own partner). Going shopping together, *social buying*, is a mission to buy something. If you pop into a cafe or bar for a drink then that is just a side issue and certainly not the actual aim. It is, of course, important for retailers to be able to make this distinction and to respond to this. It is clear that with *social buying* the ORCA model is applied fully, but it happens so quickly that it is not even clear that all four steps have actually been taken. This will often happen subconsciously and impulsively.

The Influence of the Internet

The Internet has also played a major role in changing our buying behaviour. These days we can find all the required information by simply typing in a search term. We can 'shop' by surfing from one site to another, and we can consult directly with random people in chat rooms and other social media. But it is also important that we can do this in the comfort of our own home with perhaps a glass of wine on the table, or while on the move with our smartphone or tablet (we may be bored or stuck in traffic). We no longer depend on shops or the expertise of the salesperson. We have actually become much more forthright (we have choices and are aware of the alternatives), as well as more expert. A great deal of information has already been found on the Internet before we actually come to a decision whether or not to buy something. Armed with this knowledge we go to a shop, perhaps to gain some extra information, or to confirm a feeling of certainty or maybe to alleviate any uncertainty. This visit to the shop is actually a verification of your feelings through the advice of an another person or by checking out the product itself. Once you feel and see the product, more senses are involved in the purchase decision, and so this possible uncertainty may be reduced. And it is this that lies at the heart of the retail sector's mistaken belief that customers use the Internet for orientation but then always come to the shop to make the purchase. And if in the end the customer does not buy in the shop it is the fault of the Internet and the low prices it offers. In the traditional buying process the shop was the place where the entire process of buying occurred with an emphasis on information and action. But now this is something the customer decides for himself. Instead of informing and persuading the customer, the salesperson now has to respond to the precise individual buying motives or customer uncertainties. The focus is no longer on selling products or services, but on the possible buying motives of the individual customers.

Another element of the Internet is the feeling that you know everything: a quick Google search and you'll have all the information. A brief search on the Internet and you know everything: there is no longer any excuse to not know the facts. You use this knowledge to make purchases, but also to communicate. If you have a particular ailment, you immediately look it up on the Internet before going to your GP. And then it is of course the GP's job to explain to you why your diagnosis is actually wrong. And when you are looking for information you can make up your mind whether it is worthwhile going to your GP first or instead going to the hospital straightaway to make an appointment with a specialist. Perhaps the GP is an unnecessary link in the chain.

This also happens in the retail sector. If a salesperson dares to disagree with you or ridicules your opinion, you will not stay long, even if the salesperson is right. You come to a shop prepared with all this knowledge and wish to be treated with respect, not to be trivialised or condescended to. What's more, the salesperson has to be more knowledgeable than you, or at the very least provide you with some extra benefits or value. And herein also lies a danger; a salesperson doesn't always know everything and has to learn to live with the fact that there are some customers who know more about a particular product or special offers than he does. There is also the problem that certain shops wish to save money and therefore hire cheaper and less well-trained and educated personnel. Here you are truly setting the cart before the horse. *This is a sure way of driving customers away from the shop.* These personnel often are not only less well informed than the customer himself, but also lack the skills of listening to the wishes of the customer, interpreting them correctly and responding to individual buying needs. The forthright and well-informed customer is a challenge for the traditional retail sector.

And yet the customer still goes to the shop, despite having been able to buy the product immediately on the Internet. The reasons for this have to be identified and taken advantage of, in a very targeted and effective manner. The situation has changed. The role of the salesperson in the buying process is different from his traditional role in the selling process. The salesperson must not only persuade, but must also, and particularly, listen and motivate.

MODERN WARFARE

In old-fashioned warfare a strategy was determined first of all, the so-called master plan. The generals, often in consultation with government leaders, if these were not the same people, determined the aims and the manner in which these aims would be realised. The plan was worked out in detail with objectives, resources (manpower and equipment), a precise briefing of what everybody had to do, who would give the orders and who would have to carry these out. 'Orders are orders', and that applied to all soldiers: a fixed hierarchy, a fixed leadership and fixed objectives. Part of the master plan was, of course, to incapacitate the enemy and eventually to conquer and destroy everything. Marketing warfare is also aimed a little at this principle, fully aimed at defeating the competition and even eliminating it. It's not surprising that Karl von Clausewitz is often referred to in relationship with marketing.

Modern warfare is no longer based on a master plan and top-down instructions that everyone has to follow. Soldiers are trained to assess the situation and to decide for themselves within acceptable boundaries what the best solution is. This strategy, situational assessment (SA), leaves it up to the person himself to make the decision, and they are trained to do so quickly. A briefing is given beforehand and a debriefing afterwards. The military personnel are considered to be capable and professional enough to be able to make assessments and decisions wherever they are and regardless of the situation. This is an example of empowerment from which marketing can learn a great deal. Let the sales people or the call centre staff make decisions regarding the best action to take in particular situations. They are, after all, involved and outspoken enough. A debriefing would then have to be carried out at the end of the day or week. Just as ZARA does.

Breakdown of the Buying Process

The customer is now looking for information on the Internet first before taking a buying decision. This has changed the buying behaviour. Here we see a breakdown of the buying process, or in other words a functional split of the information and buying moment. Information and buying are no longer integrated during the buying moment, such as was the case in traditional buying. Acquiring information and buying occurred together in the shop. The salesperson was the confidant, who both provided the information and persuaded the customer to buy the product. A split has now occurred between orientation and acquiring information on the one hand and buying on the other. This split is so fundamental that the retail sector has become confused and now has an identity problem.

Through Google, brand manufacturers and comparison sites (such as Kelkoo) information is acquired, products are compared and choices made. If a product is not included in the selection process, then the chances are very slim that the consumer will buy it. It is therefore understandable that everyone wants to be at the top of a Google search or to come top as the best product in the comparison sites. This search for information takes place when it best suits the customer, therefore often in the evening at home, whilst relaxing on the sofa. As a result, the selection moment is radically different from what it used to be when the customer was in the shop itself. The customer now looks for information much more freely than when he used to look around the shop. The impulses are therefore no longer dictated solely by the salesperson, who would only mention those aspects that would encourage a purchase, but can now come from anywhere. A negative review or comment on Twitter is enough for a person to decide to buy another product or go to another shop. This information process can now no longer be controlled by manufacturers or retailers; it can only be monitored. There is a clear split between products and shops. After all, the customer looks first for products and only then does he decide where to buy it. This offers new opportunities for brand manufacturers, but also leads to other options in the choice of shops.

This breakdown of the buying process and the change of the moment at which customers make their choice are important for the strategy of the retailer, but also for manufacturers and brands. What information is given and how is it given? And how will potential buyers be able to get into contact with it? In the traditional approach the shop was the place where the customer made his choice on the basis of a (usually) wide range of products. This is logical, because information provision, product comparison and buying occurred at the same time. However, this is now no longer the case. It is only once a customer has gone through his orientation process, acquired information and made a choice that he will decide independently regarding the purchase. In this decision he will be guided by many factors such as trust, delivery time/availability, impulse/emotion, convenience, price and often many other factors. The shop is nearby, the customer can see and feel the product, and take it home straightway. The webshop is directly accessible 24/7, has clear terms of delivery regarding payment and exchange (home-shopping guarantee hallmark) and can deliver quickly to the home (tomorrow). This is a personal consideration, but in both cases a product choice has already been made and only the delivery, the actual transaction, has to be decided upon. Who will best respond to the customer's personal wishes?

The New Living Environment

The living environment of customers, our lives, has changed and become much larger. Foreign countries used to be far away, but have suddenly all come within our reach. Behaviour, views and products from abroad are casually adopted or copied. There are, of course, language and cultural barriers, but seeing is believing, and that also applies to products from foreign suppliers. Particularly when websites are also available in other languages or products are modified according to the local preferences, customers no longer make a distinction between national and foreign suppliers. Quite often the customer does not even realise the product has come from abroad. Amazon.com delivers to countries worldwide as quickly as most local webshops. Customised shirts may not be made locally in a particular country, but they can still be supplied via a webshop from that country. We increasingly make less of a distinction between foreign suppliers, foreign brands and even foreign cultures. If a product, website or shop grabs our attention, then we accept this on rational grounds. If the price is right, the atmosphere appeals to us and the service meets our expectations, why should it matter whether the product comes from our country or abroad?

SWEET DREAM OF GLOBAL PROFITS

Global sourcing, or purchasing across the world and supplying via the Internet, is a new concept. Thanks to new communication possibilities and efficient logistics these days it is easy to buy products in countries where you have contacts. It is also easy to offer these products on your own website in order to sell them on again, to anyone, anywhere. This is no longer the reserve of large companies; smaller businesses can now easily do this themselves. An example of this is www.duvetandpillowwarehouse.co.uk. Duvets and bed sheets are bought in China, India, Hungary and Pakistan and then offered and sold via the website to customers throughout Europe.[1]

Or the website www.x-originals.nl selling top-class women's shawls of Pasmina and silk in Europe direct from Nepal, leather bags from Spain and Italy but all delivered within a few days throughout Europe, fully guaranteed.

Our own network of friends and acquaintances also includes people from different ethnic backgrounds, and we certainly don't make a great deal of fuss about this so long as they are fun and pleasant to be with. In actual fact, these foreign influences enrich our lives. An example of this is the rapid growth of Facebook. Particularly young people switched to Facebook in vast numbers. Perhaps this was due to their foreign friends or simply because it seemed more cool. The fact that users chose an American supplier, which may handle the information in a way that is different and even less desirable than in their own country, was not a consideration. We are individuals who wish to belong to something and retain some control over our lives. We look one another up, make friends and share activities with one another when and how we want to.

This behaviour is strongly influenced by one's environment and the personal wish for bonding or social interaction. We used to take this for granted, because we lived in fixed structures in fixed groups such as families, towns and religious communities. Social interaction is a human characteristic. In the past this used to be taken for granted, whereas these days it is up to the individual. The choice of doing something together or looking someone up is an individual one, and can be referred to as *grouping*. These groups (consisting of at least two people) are formed around a particular type of behaviour, desired activity or desired bonding. If you want to belong to a certain group, you do this deliberately and modify your behaviour to that of the group. This behaviour then immediately determines the group identity. And so in similar fashion a group of users can

---

1   Source: *Daily Telegraph*, 26 April 2011.

determine the identity of a product or brand. Lonsdale is perhaps the most striking example of this. As soon as ultra-right youths started to wear Lonsdale jeans, Lonsdale became the identification mark of ultra-right youths. So if you were a right-wing extremist, you wore Lonsdale. And, conversely, Lonsdale was suddenly confronted with an undesired brand identity. As a result, control over the brand was lost. The only options available were keeping a close eye on it and waiting until the situation changed (some degree of mild control is of course always possible). People want to have a sense of belonging. Increasingly often we see a lack of bonding with work colleagues, friends or family. Each year the number of single people and one-man businesses is on the rise, while we see a decrease in the number of physical friendships forming a social framework. We see a social impoverishment, which is one of the reasons that people look for contacts via social media, brand identification and other forms of grouping.

IN THE NETHERLANDS THE NUMBER OF PEOPLE LIVING ALONE IS ON THE RISE

The Hague – in the Netherlands – sees increasing numbers of people live alone. This has emerged from data from Statistics Netherlands (CBS).

The number of people living alone is steadily on the rise. In 2012, 1.8 million people between the ages of 18 and 65 lived alone. In 1995 this was 1.4 million. This increase is the greatest amongst middle-aged men. One reason for this is that men tend to leave the household and live on their own once their relationship breaks down and children are involved.

According to figures from Statistics Netherlands, in 2010 one in five men between the ages of 18 and 65 lived alone. This compared with just over one in six women of the same age group.

RELATIONSHIP

A quarter of those people living alone in 2010 were in a relationship. Young people tend to be single the least often. Fifty per cent of women between the ages of 18 and 25 living alone were in a steady relationship compared with four in ten men in the same age group. The percentage of middle-aged single people living alone was significantly higher. In this group, of people aged 40 to 65 just under two in ten men and women were in a steady relationship.[2]

---

2   Source: ANP 6 June 2011.

Grouping

What typifies the current behaviour is the phenomenon of *grouping*. Here the behaviour is built around personal identification and a wish for association, the group identification. In the traditional approach groups were formed around intended target groups, specified with objective characteristics such as gender, age, income and background. This allowed segments to be formed for which products were made. At the foundation of this lay the assumption that a specific behaviour arose based on these objective characteristics. After all, women behave differently to men, don't they, and income determines what you do? These days this is a clear misconception.

The confusion arose when the behaviour, influenced by the communication industry and later the Internet, became increasingly more individual. The social changes also stimulated this development. In the 1980s we were surprised about the atypical behaviour of many young people, but also about the 'new' elderly who did their best to remain young: running, and going to fitness centres and discos. These were the first signals of a behaviour-controlled identification, based on a personal wish for association. At the moment people are allowing themselves to be heavily influenced by this group identity, which is based upon behaviour and with which everyone can associate themselves irrespective of age, gender or ethnic background. The hype surrounding the iPad is perhaps a good example of this. Through the iPad you belong to a particular group of computer users with a common identity of being young, dynamic, modern and always *connected*; it does not matter whether you are actually young or old. If you then have a netbook (a small computer with limited functionality), which can perhaps do the same, you don't quite fit in. The same applies, of course, to users of the Samsung Galaxy and other tablets. They often justify their choices on rational grounds; after all, when it comes to emotional value Apple's iPad is unbeatable (at the moment). From a technical point of view, however, a lot can be said for choosing a device with the *open android system*, which is used by the Samsung Galaxy, instead of the closed iOS system used by Apple.

Grouping is built around individual behaviour. By regarding this behaviour as the core element, a group composed of like-minded people arises, who do and want the same thing. The traditional approach involves forming groups that are based on objective characteristics, whereas with *grouping* a group consisting of like-minded people arises through identical behaviour. This is extremely relevant to the buying process; after all, you have to regard your customers as a group of like-minded people. The behaviour determines the buying motives, or, in other words: identical buying motives determine the group.

An iPad is not bought on rational grounds. One should therefore not evaluate this product on rational grounds, just as one should not evaluate a Samsung Galaxy on emotional grounds (but rather on rational considerations). The buying motives for both products are essentially different, so the selling arguments should also be different. The information process of the customer will also be different and the product chosen on different grounds. For consumers, however, there is a deeper reason behind this change in how groups are formed. Of course people want to be recognised and accepted as individuals. It is a response to the regulated society. They want to be themselves and set themselves apart as individuals. Based on this intrinsic need, they search for an environment where this is possible and they accept behaviour that facilitates and stimulates this. This drives away any feelings of solitude or uncertainty, which is always inherent in individualism. We can now be an individual within the group framework in relation to the rest of the world, but without the feeling of solitude, and that gives much more security – the same sense of security that we used to have within our living environment, the family, school or our neighbourhood. This gives a sense of security, attachment and a warm group feeling.

An iPad user does not wish to be seen as a computer user, just as the iPhone to its user is not just a mobile phone. It is a token of individuality and character, as well as a sign that you are open to change. In this way, you set yourself apart from others, whilst you still feel the solidarity of your peers.

The iPad and iPhone of Apple

These 'new' groups arise as like-minded people with the same behaviour feel some connection with one another. This group may appear like a homogeneous entity, but that's certainly not the case. It is merely a group of individuals who have something in common. It was easy with groups based on objective characteristics, as an objective characteristic is clearly visible and the behaviour therefore predictable. People on a high income tend to buy certain types of clothes, live in a particular type of house and drive a particular type of car. But an iPad user only has the iPad as the common factor with like-minded people; apart from that their behaviour can be completely different.

For this group formation one has to look for a common denominator, something that everyone has in common with one another, in the behaviour that leads to purchasing an iPad. This common denominator can, of course, be the affection for the Apple brand, but also a need to set oneself apart. The iPad is then regarded as a means to achieve this objective. This common denominator is important for suppliers, as it determines the interpretation of the information that is being sought. It isn't so much about what an iPad can do, it's about its social status. That is why a supplier has to provide information other than, for example, technical details or information regarding its ease-of-use. This applies to brands and products as well as to the retailer.

Social Media

This group formation is based on behaviour and is usually of a temporary nature. Sharing an activity or wearing or buying something whereby you can set yourself apart in some way or another is determined by a particular moment or is perhaps important in a particular phase. Other products will come along whereby you can again set yourself apart, or perhaps you no longer wish to be associated with that particular group. A more fundamental aspect is a wish to be part of a social network. This helps to form a foundation to your life. This was traditionally a network of family members, friends and acquaintances whom you knew personally. The world was orderly and close at hand, but that is no longer the case. Due to increased mobility, our – physical – living environment has grown to such an extent that it has become much less orderly. As there are also many more choices available than previously, both concerning the products offered and the financial possibilities open to you, the individual behaviour makes sense. This individualism, however, has spurred on the feeling of solitude again, and that is something you want to avoid. Group formation, however, provides a possibility of doing something about it and the Internet provides a solution with social media. Although there are many forms of social media, each with their own objective and possibilities, in this respect these social networks are particularly important. Through these networks we show that we truly want to keep in contact with others, our 'friends' and connections.

Facebook is an example of a social network whereby we look one another up and share experiences. We tell others what we are doing, what our hobbies are and share photos and clips. What we do, in fact, is let others take a peek into our lives, whilst we in turn follow the lives of others. The basic need involved here is, of course, a feeling of bonding, belonging, but also a need for looking and sharing. Voyeurism and exhibitionism still form, also with the modern media, part of our behaviour. We used to enjoy not only prying on and gossiping about others (voyeurism), but also setting ourselves apart from the rest with our particular clothes, cars and the way we would spend money (exhibitionism).

This worked well within the limitations of the physical environment, our town or our neighbourhood. However, today we use different means – the social networks.

Children go on Internet to play with other children in special child-friendly social media sites like Habbo Hotel and to get to know one another. Thanks to the anonymity of computer use in combination with an avatar that you can select yourself, you can anonymously watch the behaviour of others, communicate with one another and make friends without ever actually meeting them. Children often have several of these avatars which can vary in gender. In this way they can experiment with a certain behaviour and attract other friends – an innocent experiment for children to discover their preferences and to determine their identity. You also see this 'mirror behaviour' in teenagers in the real world, but then the interaction is not anonymous as it is with an avatar. Due to the often direct, but anonymous, contacts and the open communication (there are fewer inhibitions), these children often regard the friendships on sites like Habbo Hotel as closer and more honest than in the real world. *It is not important what you look like, but who you are!*

Habbo Hotel is a conditioned environment whereby an identity check is necessary to become a member. This helps to prevent undesirable situations. There is an age restriction (only children) and behaviour is monitored. This helps to make it a safe environment.

For teenagers of around 16 years of age there are the social networks. Here they can share things. You're no longer anonymous. The need for voyeurism and exhibitionism now becomes clearer. You want to show who you are and what you're up to, but you want to look at others as well. There is a strong desire to keep in contact. On your wall you can post messages, respond to other people's messages and upload photos, thereby giving people a peek into your life. This gives rise to the feeling of belonging, of taking part in a network of friends, but it also provides a way of testing out one's own behaviour. These days people have considerably fewer physical friends than people used to have, but the wish to belong and the need for bonding certainly has not got any less. Networks such as Facebook have a strong binding character, and initially commercial applications did not seem to naturally fit in with their ethos. These networks show you in your private life. Commercial messages are therefore often regarded as an irritation. For other social networks such as Twitter or YouTube this is less of a problem. Commercial applications are possible, providing the wishes of the users of the social media are taken into account and potential irritations are avoided. If irritations do occur, they should be dealt with straightaway.

The use of social media has now become part of marketing strategy. A recent British study indicated that in 2010 companies spent about 20% of their marketing budget on social media.

The study[3] reveals that worldwide more companies are using social media as a channel to maintain contact with existing customers and to inform them (52%). The financial crisis has led to companies in all sectors taking a more critical look at the traditional working methods, from supply chain management, leaner working methods and cloud computing to more intensive use of video communication and the use of new marketing tools. An increasing numbers of companies are using new channels to increase the loyalty of existing customers and to recruit new customers. As many as 17% of the users of social networks are either a fan, follower or friend of a business page or profile.

Social Individualism

In addition to a social network for your private contacts there are also networks for business contacts. LinkedIn and Plaxo are two such examples. All these social media are a form of social individualism. We all want to do the things we enjoy and want to be recognised as individuals. However, we also have a need to belong, a need for social contact. The development of social individualism has intensified as the traditional group formation, as described above, began to become less important. This occurred hand in hand with the adoption of new possibilities. The telephone enabled us to keep in contact with friends, family and acquaintances without having to see them face to face. The Internet, however, has taken this a step further. You can share your life with others without actually having met physically. And yet the feeling of the group, of friendship and belonging is by no means less. Our need for communication can also be fulfilled in another way. This manner of group formation, whereby you can choose with whom you are friends and the group to which you want to belong, in combination with the possibility of communicating with the group or members of the group, is a form of social individualism.

In the physical world this process began in the 1980s, when we saw a greater mobility and a sharp rise in individualism. Friendships increasingly

---

3   Source: CMOs on Social Marketing, Bazaarvoice, 2011. Study commissioned by Regus with the title *Social Recovery, a Global Survey of Business Use of Social Networks*, June 2011. The study was carried out by Marketing UK among 17,000 representatives of companies from the Regus network.

involved sharing an activity, sport, music or simply shopping with one another. And often with different people who also enjoyed these activities. The 1990s saw a breakthrough in new media in the form of the Internet and mobile telephones. This led to an increase in people communicating, and in a different manner: from person to person, whenever it was desired. A growing need for communication arose. Young people no longer switched off their mobile phones. They wanted to be able to be reached by their friends and acquaintances at all times. What followed were the possibilities offered by the Internet, again from person to person. Chatting, blogging, sending emails and text messages all became part of one's daily contact. The 1990s were a continuation of the 1980s in terms of individualism, but then with the addition of social wishes and social contacts. The combination of this individualism and the communication needs of the 1990s led to the social individualism that we see today. This is now supplemented by the contacts offered by social media such as Facebook, whereby people have strong connections. And this also applies to Twitter, where the types of connections are different yet again, but where you still share part of your life with your followers. This social individualism enables you to make a conscious choice regarding the group to which you want to belong, the people you accept as friends and the activities you want to share. A freedom of choice and freedom regarding the extent of the commitment.

Our behaviour has radically changed due to the changes in society, the changes in our own lives and the influence of the Internet. The logical choice of shopping in the neighbourhood has disappeared as a result. We can now decide where and when we shop based on our personal wishes and preferences. This behaviour leads to a different type of buying behaviour and consequently also to changes in retail. Internet sales are continuing to increase, irrespective of the consumers' age, gender or other criteria. The retail sector has a great challenge ahead of it whereby it can respond effectively to the changes and determine its future. Will physical shops still be necessary in the future? And if so, what should they look like? Is the Internet a solution alongside the physical shop, a so-called multi-channel concept or a *click and mortar concept*, or should we perhaps look for other solutions like mobile Internet? The retail sector is faced with a critical decision: adapt or stop altogether!

BEST BUY IS TAKING A FRESH LOOK

Best Buy, the largest American electronics retailer, is busy taking a fresh look into how best to attract customers and the most effective way of responding to the new way of shopping – ambassadors speaking to customers in the shop and demonstrating new gadgets, the *connected store concept*, or a price that can vary per day depending on the competition, eagerness to buy, or purely because the customers want this. Brian Dunn, CEO, is counting on a good service as the strategic weapon and a similar price level to discounters. Profits can then also be made with *add-ons*, eye-catching gadgets, visible and there to be touched and held. The salespeople are trained to demonstrate the gadgets properly. Not only does this help to create emotion, but the sales staff are able to provide immediate service and refer customers to the relevant accessories. But the Internet has also come into the shop in the form of touch screen kiosks, which make it possible to order the product directly online (and then a little while later to collect it at the cash desk), print out reviews or simply compare prices. According to Dunn, women in particular are impressed by this shop, as it is well organised and orderly.

Conclusion and Summary of Chapter 2

The developments that influence retail in the future have three dimensions: the relationship of suppliers (manufacturers) and retailers, the new buying behaviour of consumers and the influence of technology.

Table 2.1   Summary and conclusion

Developments of influence	Supplier/ manufacturer	New buying behaviour	Technology
Developments separate within current structure of retailing.	Sell directly, build strong brands, supply internationally under the same conditions.	Buying on the Internet and in the shop. Well-informed, driven by the moment. Less loyalty. Attachment to brands, *social grouping* behaviour.	Accessible everywhere, open standards. Integration of video and later *augmented reality*. Integration physical and online. Mobile telephones and tablets linked to apps are the future.
Consequences for current structure.	Channel conflict and loss of mutual dependency.	Falling property value, pressure on margins, reorganisation of traditional retail.	*Customer driven*, transparency in product range, different balance rationale/emotion and offline-online, influence of social networks, disaggregation of the purchase.

3

Is There Still a Future for Shops? The Battle Has Commenced, with Suppliers, Customers and the Internet

The retailer has to fight at different fronts simultaneously in order to secure a future. He has to fight against Internet sales as well as the changed buying behaviour of customers. They now place different demands on shops such as extended opening hours (Sundays), more knowledgeable sales staff and a different experience in the shop. The retailer has to fight against suppliers who were his partners for years but now see opportunities to sell to customers directly and who are not averse to trampling on the retailers. He has to fight against Internet suppliers who are often cheaper and who can deliver to people's homes. Due to these changes the actual role, the function and the very existence of the (physical) shop is now open to question. The retailer also has to fight against the government which does not seem very willing to help shopkeepers in these difficult times. The shopkeeper has to look for new possibilities to provide a service to customers such as offering Wi-Fi, apps or *location-based services*, or perhaps even free transport to shopping centres or home delivery and personal shopping assistance.

An initial response of the current shopkeepers to the popularity of webshops was to try to eliminate this new competition or in any case to paint them as unreliable. Will the orders actually arrive? How do you know they are the right products? Can you exchange them? Can you get your money back? These types of questions created uncertainty. However, it was only when the webshops continued growing that shopkeepers started to consider whether their own proposition perhaps had to change. And that is where we are now, in 2012. All these changes and the retailers' response to them will determine the future of the current retail trade. But is there still a future for the existing retail trade and where will they be located, in town, out of town or in shopping malls?

A Different Buying Behaviour a Threat to Shops

Shops are stuck in their traditional role of local service provider. Customers never used to have any other choice but to buy in their neighbourhood. Shops were the local sales point. Shops later came together to form purchasing groups, which provided retailers with financial, marketing and purchasing services. Good retailing was associated with a sound purchasing policy, good product choice, pleasant premises and attractive prices. Joint purchasing led to better conditions, and therefore also to improved margins and competitive pricing.

This approach worked as long as customers bought in a certain area and the other shops in the area formed the competition. The prices could be easily compared by customers and retailers alike. Shopkeepers knew one another and were aware of one another's strong and weak points. Retailing was clear and very much based upon the products being sold. The retailer's strength lay in a good cost price, a suitable location, a good product range and pleasant sales staff. In an ideal situation there was a local network; if customers knew the retailer themselves then they would be happy to provide him with their custom and money. And as an extra, there was always the property itself. As long as the shopping street remained attractive to customers the value of premises there increased each year.

Retail Value Drivers

The book *Inside the Mind of the Shopper*[1] comprehensively explains how the retail focus is shifting. The traditional business model consists of four cornerstones:

1.   the margins of the trade, such as bonuses

2.   the interest on cash, buy now pay later

---

1   Herb Sorensen, 2009, *Inside the Mind of the Shopper*, Upper Saddle River, NJ: Pearson Education, pp. 18, 19, 114.

3.   the property

4.   the margin on transactions

Traditional retailers still think along the lines of these four value components. They think that if profits made on transactions decline there is still no cause for concern; after all, their property still retains its value. Cash flow is also an important component. However, in the last few years there has been a negative development on all fronts of these value elements: businesses no longer sell only via shops, but now also use the Internet. The margin has come under pressure due to products also being offered from abroad, the well-informed consumer and the lower prices offered on the Internet. The turnover rate of the products has declined, with a negative influence on cashflow. What's more, interest rates have been at a historical low for a number of years now. And to top it all, property prices have been declining whereby business properties that greatly depend upon the location have shown a sharper decrease than those in the (private) housing market. The only thing that is then left is the transaction margin, and this has constantly come under pressure due to the critical, well-informed consumer. All in all, a worrying development for the retail trade, which is resulting in empty shops in town centres, villages and old hopping precincts.

Table 3.1   Development of traditional 'profit drivers'

Traditional profit makers for retail (*value drivers*)	Applications	Development
Trade margins, bonus.	Dependent on the sector, strong in food and electronics.	Rapid reduction for traditional retail due to the Internet as new sales channel.
Interest on cash.	Strong in food.	Rapid reduction due to low interest rates and more stringent payment conditions.
Property.	Non-food retail.	Rapid reduction due to empty properties in traditional shopping streets and centres.
Margin on transactions.	All segments.	Reduction due to international supply of products, the Internet and new buying behaviour of consumers.

The traditional profit *drivers* of physical retail are rapidly reducing in value. The retail trade has to reconsider once more what possibilities there are to make profit, and again look for *value drivers* and profit sources: who is willing to pay for what?

The mutual dependency between retailers and suppliers led to a mutual respect. Customers were collectively attracted by a pleasant shopping street or shopping centre, or by joint activities such as fairs or fashion shows or by tempting discounts. This mutual dependency is now under pressure due to the new buying behaviour shown by customers. Their decision process is no longer transparent; each customer chooses in his or her own way. This puts the retail trade under pressure. The lower prices offered by the Internet are usually given as the reason behind the declining sales, but that's not quite true. The price on the Internet is transparent. The customer, however, buys a product for personal reasons, and price may be an important criterion, but not necessarily. The retail trade has to look again at its appeal and the specific buying motives of customers. Responding to this new buying behaviour is therefore essential for its continued existence. Also location is increasingly important. Customers like to shop where it adds value: run shopping should be efficient (or Internet), fun shopping should be pleasant with good parking facilities, and catering.

Traditional Sales Criteria for Shops

Customers have always bought in shops that lie within their mobile action radius. In the twentieth century this choice was fairly straightforward – namely, a local shop that was easily accessible. Occasionally people used mail-order companies. In the first case we refer to traditional retail (shopping 1.0), whereas in the second case we refer to direct retail or mail ordering (shopping 2.0). It was only in the 1990s that we saw any major change to this due to the arrival of the Internet. The customer's behaviour also changed, not only as a result of the Internet, but also due to other factors such as the customer's increased mobility, a different way of spending and perceiving leisure time and a different type of group formation.

What do women between the ages of 19 and 33 want?

54.2% of women want to shop for clothes on their own, the rest like to do this together with a family member or girlfriend.

79.2% of women ask their girlfriends for advice when shopping.

20.8% of women do not consider another person's advice regarding fashion or clothes important when shopping.

92.7% of women are extremely influenced by fashion experts or news about fashion.

58.3% of women read about fashion in magazines or on blogs.

91.7% of women buy in a physical shop. The most important products then are electronics, books and magazines, clothes and accessories.

66.7% of women search for fashion articles and reports online.[2]

The traditional sales criteria of shops are changing as buying behaviour changes. The retailer has to adapt and respond to these changes in the new buying behaviour and compete using new possibilities such as the Internet. These traditional sales criteria consisted of:

- the location

- the product range

- the availability of products

- the information in the shop

- the look and feel

- the sales staff

THE LOCATION

For shopkeepers it was important to have a location that was attractive to the public and to have the appropriate price ratio per square metre. For supermarkets the parking facilities and the available square metres were important, whereas for other types of shops critical factors were the look and feel of the location, having other shops in the vicinity and the accessibility of the shop to customers and suppliers. Especially a popular shop in the neighbourhood was important as a magnet for all shops. Sometimes this was a supermarket, but also a major department store, shop with sporting equipment or a low price shop was possible.

---

2   Study carried out by students among 780 women between the ages of 19 and 33 in March 2011.

THE PRODUCT RANGE

The product range comprised of items and brands that were related to the particular sector, and so related to one another. With a dress, for example, there could be a matching scarf, belt or jewellery. In the case of electronics, there would be the *supplies* and components. The product range was clearly sector and product oriented, making it easy for customers to buy matching accessories. In other words, you buy foodstuffs in the supermarket and electrical products and components in an electronics shop. For a shop it was (and is) important that the customer has a choice, a variety of articles should be available. If a customer knows exactly what to buy, Internet is a logical alternative.

THE AVAILABILITY OF PRODUCTS

The availability of products means here that you can see and feel the products and take them home. For a customer this is an important criterion, as you can determine for yourself whether a product is good, or whether the price/quality ratio is acceptable and whether the product meets expectations. The fact that you can take the products home with you straightaway is important, as buying is also desiring, a wish to possess. And if this wish to possess is not immediately fulfilled then it usually results in a feeling of disappointment. You want it, and you want it now. This wish to possess also plays a role when it comes to having the product delivered to your door. So the sooner it can be delivered, the better.

THE INFORMATION IN THE SHOP

In a shop you expect expertise and advice. The salesperson has to assist you in the purchase by providing objective advice based on knowledge and a personal opinion. If a salesperson cannot answer a particular question, then this can be disappointing; it undermines the trust the customer has in the shop and in the salesperson in particular. Therefore it is sad to see that retailers have replaced good, well-informed staff with cheap temporary staff because of staffing costs. A wrong decision.

THE LOOK AND FEEL

The look and feel is also important. Does the shop come across as fun, clean and orderly or does it appear hectic and sloppy? The look and feel is important as it helps to attract customers and is part of the expectations. The look and feel must therefore be in line with these expectations. That means a luxurious look and feel for luxury items, but different look and feel if you want to come across as inexpensive or customer friendly.

THE SALES STAFF

The sales staff have to be helpful, knowledgeable in their particular area, friendly and above all willing to help you in the decision-making and buying process. For this it is important that the sales person and customer complement one another, that the sales person not just shows off his product knowledge but asks clear questions in order to help the customer in the decision-making process. For the customer it sometimes feels as if you have to pay for the sales staff's attention and smiles. Friendly, helpful staff are an asset to every store.

All these sales criteria were important for the retailer in acquiring a place among the shopping public. Over the last few years this buying behaviour has become more individual. Customers are now much more critical and tend to think carefully when buying. It is therefore logical that there are other reasons, often personal ones, which determine where a product is bought. As these days customers have a full understanding and knowledge of the products on offer, they are free to cherry-pick. This means that they will only use those sales criteria (benefits) which the retailer possesses. As a result, customers will show less loyalty towards a particular shop and look for special offers. Customers used to be able to choose from just a few shops in the area, but with the new buying behaviour this has changed.

Customers now have a much greater choice. Based on this new buying behaviour it is possible that the customer will first look around on the Internet but eventually still buy in the shop. The reverse is also possible. The shopkeeper has to provide advice and show the item, but the customer may then walk out and buy the item online, and possibly more cheaply. A conflict has arisen between the retailer's information function and the sales/buying function – a frustrating situation of course, as the retailer provides information and service but ends up earning nothing. This is further exacerbated by the fact that the customer has acquired so much information on the Internet which then also creates conflict as the retailer has to compete with that as well. At the end of the day it can no longer be taken for granted that someone will buy in a physical shop; the choice of whether to buy in a physical shop has now become a choice that people are able to consider.

The Response to the New Buying Behaviour of Customers

The first response of the traditional retailers to the new buying behaviour was to play down the influence of the Internet:

How do you know that the online orders will actually arrive? I hear so many negative stories about this. Do you actually know the supplier? They are often based abroad, way out in Outer Mongolia. Service and guarantee? Forget it! They are unreliable suppliers. Yes, you first have to pay and then wait and see, but don't expect to be able to change the items or get your money back from these folks.

In recent years, however, people have had far more positive experiences and increasingly started to buy online. Retailers initially thought that these online shoppers were primarily young people; the older generation would surely continue to come to the physical shops. 'They have been doing so for decades, so why should this suddenly change?'

This trivialisation of the changes has now turned into a challenge. The number of visitors going to shops and shopping centres has dropped in recent years, while Internet sales have been increasing considerably for a number of years now.

> Figures from the Organisation for Economic Co-operation and Development (OECD) show that six out of ten British adults use the internet to buy products such as food, clothing, music or holidays. This is twice the average of the OECD's 34 member states, which include the US, Germany, Australia and France. On average, just three out of ten people in OECD nations buy goods or services online. Britons spent £68.2 billion on the internet last year, an increase of almost £10 billion on 2010, according to IMRG, a body which represents the UK's online retailers. This is equivalent to £2,180 for every adult in the country.[3]

It has also been recognised that the impact of the Internet influences not only buying (the transactions), but the entire buying process. The 'new buying' is a totally different shopping experience whereby the customer makes a conscious choice for either the Internet or the physical shop and whereby looking around and obtaining information are separate to the actual buying.

---

3   James Hall, *Daily Telegraph*, 1 February 2012.

The Realisation That Something Has to Change

The first step in the change process is to think carefully about the reasons why customers come to shops and why they choose to buy either on the Internet or in the shop itself. In the shop the buying occurred at the same time as the obtaining of information, and so selling products was a question of informing well and selling effectively using the appropriate selling points. Now customers make a conscious decision when going to a shop for very specific reasons: they go to buy something, or for information, for the service or just to be able to see the products.

Now that customers have a choice, a retailer has to be aware of the reasons why customers come to the shop. Customers can buy anything on the Internet, yet they still come to the shop, often very deliberately and for specific individual reasons. It is these very reasons that are important when determining whether the shop has a future. What can these reasons be?

In the shop customers expect expert knowledge, reliability or service. In addition, customers can see, feel and experience the product (perhaps try it on). And then they can take it straight home. These are all clear advantages over the Internet. Other reasons can be the product range and the possibility of choosing and comparing with what a shop always offers. Retailing is often also a *people business*, granting the shop your custom, the pleasant contact with the sales staff and the personal advice. The customers' feelings about it should also be good and correspond with the expectations, rational considerations or emotions, help in the purchase or self-service. The look and feel of a shop and how a person experiences it have to meet the expectations and wishes of the buying public. Sometimes customers just want to have a look around, take in the atmosphere and look for ideas. Retailers should respond to this by providing inspiration or the experience, the layout, music, a coffee corner, and so on; simply treat the visitors and customers, surprise them. Shopping is a leisure activity. As customers seldom come for just one shop, but for a collection of shops or a concept, there has to be a certain appeal that is supported by the other shops: the environment, the attractiveness of the city, a shop in the neighbourhood, an attraction or other environmental factors that can act as a magnet (for example an electronics shop next to a football stadium is particularly appealing to men).

Customers do not suddenly change their behaviour. This is usually a slow process. Some changes only come about if there is an urgent necessity. This necessity is usually not present, unless the local shop closes down and you have no other choice but to buy online. In most other cases this is a gradual process where there are always plenty of opportunities for the retailer. A retailer may also benefit from looking at the advantages and disadvantages of this change. The shop can create some sort of extra benefit at a certain moment in the buying behaviour, for example when the customer makes a purchase or is just looking around. In the physical shop products can be touched and taken home straightaway. It is also possible to add extra experiences for the customer, as is done in the Nike shops or the shops of Abercrombie and Fitch. The traditional retail sector has not yet lost out to the new buying behaviour, but it does have to look closely at the reasons that customers go to shops, and take advantage of them. This in turn would motivate customers to make the decision to go to the shop.

The Battle between Suppliers and Shops

For decades suppliers and manufacturers were the partner of the retailer. One party manufactured the products and the other one sold them. A supplier has a strong focus on the product and wishes to be distinctive in relation to other products, whereas retailers focus strongly on the customer and wish to set themselves apart from other shops. This clear role division has now come under pressure due to the new possibilities. As customers also have a preference for a particular brand or product which is sometimes stronger than the preference for a shop, suppliers have developed a certain position of power. Thanks to the new buying behaviour of customers and the role of the Internet, in the last few years it has become increasingly easier to identify customers and also to maintain direct contact with them. Building up an address database is a simple matter, and it is easy to communicate directly by letter or email. The question, however, is whether manufacturers do indeed communicate directly with customers and then refer them to a shop where other brands are sold as well. Direct sales by suppliers have become an alternative, thereby unleashing the competition with the retailer. In order to avoid such battles very clear agreements have to be made as was done by Miele. Miele will deal with all Internet sales on behalf of the retailers. In place of the normal bonus they will receive a lower bonus but all deliveries are done by Miele, a close cooperation on Internet and a normal supplier-retailer relationship in the shop (e.g. as practised in Germany and the Netherlands).

Something Going On in the Channel: Manufacturer versus the Shopkeeper

It can no longer be taken for granted that people will buy from a physical shop. It is therefore understandable that manufacturers are now questioning why they should still have to sell through shops rather than offer the products directly. In fact this is already happening in many cases, such as with Apple, Sony, Esprit and State of Art. An interesting conflict has arisen between (brand) manufacturers and shopkeepers. It is a battle for the preference of the customer; will the customer buy a product (brand) or will he buy at the shop? This conflict has a number of dimensions:

- Product brand or shop brand: which is the stronger?

- Who has customer ownership and who has the best bond with the customer?

- What purchase choice does a customer make: buying at home or in the shop?

- What are the best conditions for buying?

Does the customer choose a product brand or a shop (as brand)? If the customer chooses a product brand, it could be that the loyalty towards the brand is greater than that towards the shop. The shop then only has limited advantages, such as the available choices and having the products in stock. Advice, buying support or product instructions are usually not necessary. The trust in the brand is so great that people buy without seeing the product. This was seen, for example, with the pre-orders for the new Apple iPad. People had not yet seen the product but still trusted that it would be good. The benefits offered by a shop have decreased greatly due to this trust in particular brands. After all, customers can buy the brand (from the manufacturer) directly. And this trust in the brand is so great that even a higher price is accepted.

This is beneficial to the manufacturer; the margin of the shopkeeper remains with the manufacturer, but an even more important benefit is the customer contact. As customers order directly, they immediately leave behind their contact information. The 'customer ownership' then lies with the manufacturer. The manufacturer is therefore able to approach the customer directly with services, other products or replacement products. In the traditional distribution model there was a functional division between the manufacturer and the retailer. The manufacturer had to deliver good products to the retailer and the retailer had to sell the products and provide good service to the customers. The customer ownership lay with the retailer. In order to influence this relationship manufacturers tried to collect the customers' addresses through the guarantee cards. The buyers of the products would then go onto the Internet to register the purchase to obtain the manufacturer's warranty. At the same time the customer would give permission to be kept informed on the latest products or other innovations. This is how for many years Electrolux collected guarantee cards on its service sites of all its Electrolux products, such as Electrolux, AEG and Zanussi.

In the case of software this registration has even become part of the product itself. By registering the purchase the buyer automatically receives new releases.

Manufacturers never used to do much with the guarantee cards or purchase registration. This was often due to the lack of knowledge regarding the power of personal communication and also because the manufacturer's focus was on supporting the retailer rather than supporting and building a relationship with individual customers. This is still the case. Retailers focus on personal contact with customers and manufacturers on the (direct) communication with retailers.

The manufacturer's marketing communication department is mainly a department that concentrates on mass communication and trade marketing, the relationship with retailers. Through mass communication manufacturers try to build brands and to create a top-of-mind position, so that customers might visit the (physical) shop to buy the products. Due to sophisticated advertising strategies in particular, certain expectations are created for a brand article (imaginary values) that lead to a preference amongst customers. The strength of the manufacturer's advertising department lies in building a brand, protecting the brand and together with the retailers ensuring that the article is presented well in the shop. When manufacturers refer to their customers, they mean the retailers and not the end customer. Manufacturers actively approach retailers (or wholesalers and buying cooperatives). Premiums, bonuses, advertising material and, for example, also study trips are used to motivate these resellers to stock and sell these products. This push strategy was the domain of the (brand) manufacturers and dictated the relationship with the retailer. It therefore makes sense that the retail sector has a strong focus on the purchasing function as a basis for a good selling proposition.

Conversely the shopkeepers have direct contact with customers, and meet more of the customer's needs than just selling them products. Customers feel a bond with the shop based on personal buying motives. Due to the relationship with the shop, the salesperson or shopkeeper, the customer feels he can trust the shop. That's why the entire buying process, from orientation to obtaining information and buying, all took place in the shop. These steps are also part of building a relationship of trust and are taken in a deliberate and well-considered manner. The feeling of trust in the shop increases and eventually the purchase is made (this process can take a few minutes up to a matter of hours, or even weeks). This is the case with a traditional buying process where the shop plays a dominant role.

As already mentioned, this has changed. After all, why would you continue to look around in a shop and search there for information if there is a strong loyalty towards a product? Manufacturers can see this as well, and respond to it by providing information on their websites and by even selling their products directly. Regular and loyal customers who tend to make well-considered purchases can then go to the manufacturer to buy, whereas the more uncertain or fickle customers go to the shop for advice. The role of the shop has therefore changed. The loyalty of faithful brand-conscious customers to the shop is under pressure, and the loyalty towards the (brand) item greater.

BEST BUY WISHES TO DOUBLE ONLINE SALES

Best Buy wishes to double its online sales within five years, reports Internet Retailer on its website. The American chain of consumer electronics is aiming to realise an online turnover of $4 billion in 2016. Within this period the surface area of the chain's physical shops, however, will have to be reduced by 10%.

The market leader in the United States has based its plans on the wishes of the customer. 'There is now a new definition for convenience; the possibility of communicating your conditions to a company,' explains vice president Shari Ballard. Investigations have revealed that 60% of the sales at the physical shops of Best Buy were first viewed online and that 40% of the online sales were collected in the shops. The online growth will be spurred on by supplying a wider choice, matching service and more digital content. What's more, the chain will open at least 350 shops that focus purely on selling mobile phones.

In the physical shops the productivity will be reinforced with experts on the shop floor and touchscreen monitors through which product information can easily be found.

Source: RetailNews.

A reassessment of the function of the (brand) manufacturer and that of the shop is the result. The battle between brand manufacturers and the retailers has only just begun. Marks & Spencer[4] (M&S) has decided to sell only its own brand, both in the shop and online on its M&S site. It is difficult to compare all aspects of a company's own brand products with those of another company. This gives rise to a monopoly position for M&S with their own brand, a battle between a manufacturer's product brand and the shop as brand.

ZARA follows a similar strategy, whereby it only sells its own brand products. These products follow the latest fashion and are often trendsetting. If you want to know what the (latest) range is, then you have to go to the ZARA shop. ZARA's product range on the Internet is still rather limited. The retail trade is fighting back against manufacturers with their own (brand) weapon. That, however, requires a strong retail formula and a strong retail brand. The shop's *value driver* has changed from a presence and distribution point to trust and customer loyalty. The battleground is the shop or the Internet, but it is also a battle between retailer, online retailer and manufacturer.

Battle for the Customer

The battle between a product brand and a shop brand is a battle for the favour of customers. It would be much better if brand manufacturers and shops were to work together to attract customers. Both parties would then be able to use one another's appeal. Quite often the shop acts as a magnet attracting foreign customers, with department stores working together with brand manufacturers by arranging the departments into sections according to brand. The men's and ladies' fashion departments of large department stores such as Bloomingdale, Macy's, El Corte Inglés and Debenhams are arranged in such a way with sections devoted to specific labels. This allows brands to position themselves very specifically and to make use of the image and traffic of the department store. Perfume departments are also arranged according to brand,

---

4   Mark Bolland, CEO of Marks & Spencer, outline of strategy, London *Evening Standard*, 24 May 2011; on www.smarta.com, 9 November 2010.

with each brand having its own counter or section in the store. The combination of brands, a dominant place in the shop and the power of pleasant fragrances attract customers to the department store and the department.

Well-known brands make the department store more attractive and give it greater prestige. This concept led to a *shop in the shop* concept. The brands rented space in the department store which then in effect became a service provider (facilitator). The brands are seen as an extra pull, helping to attract even more people to the shop, which benefits the total sales. This concept was and still is very successful, but also leads to a stronger customer loyalty towards (product) brands. If this product brand becomes stronger, manufacturers will end up opening their own shops and perhaps also closing down their sections in these large stores. Nike, Apple and Garmin, as well as many labels from the fashion world are examples of this, such as Esprit, Gap, Dior and Lanvin. These brand shops often search one another out in certain streets, such as the PC Hooftstraat in Amsterdam, Bond Street in London and Rodeo Drive in Los Angeles, thereby giving these areas a more exclusive character. This attracts customers to these streets which in turn creates a different image from the rest of the shopping area and, consequently leads to more custom. The brand manufacturers are now battling directly with their old distribution channel, the shops. This will lead to a reduction of the brand value of the department store and a stronger image of the brand, whilst the role and function of the shop as a result will be undermined. The options available to customers in the shop will decrease, whilst the shop's appeal will erode as strong brands will no longer be sold there. The role that the shop has in choosing products will as a result increasingly deteriorate, whilst this was actually one of its most important weapons.

HIGH STREETS 'LACK THE RECOVERY FACTOR'

A total of 11pc more property agents reported a fall in interest from retailers rather than a rise compared with the final quarter of 2011, according to the latest commercial market survey from the Royal Institution of Chartered Surveyors (RICS). The declining demand is despite the number of empty shops on high streets already being at record levels of more than 14pc. The survey dampens hopes of a recovery in the retail property market.

Source: Graham Ruddick, *Daily Telegraph*, 6 April 2012.

The battle between product and shop brands and that between manufacturers and retailers will continue to rage fiercely in the coming years. The victors will be determined by their actions and responses to one another. It will be clear in Chapter 4 that the battle in the distribution channel will also lead to other possibilities and other business models. But ultimately it is the customer and his behaviour that will determine the future.

The battle that is taking place between manufacturer and retailer is a battle for the customer, a battle for the favour and the *share of wallet* of the customer. As we have seen, the customer chooses on the basis of personal preferences, whatever they may be. This preference, however, can be influenced by an effective communication strategy. It is therefore important to have direct contact with the customer. For the traditional shopkeeper and the traditional buying process this is simple: the customer comes into the shop. It is then possible to enter into a dialogue with the customer and convince him that the decision to buy is the right one. But the shop also acquires a top-of-mind position, as the customer regularly walks past the shop. Every time a customer sees a shop, hears its name or reads about it, a mnemonic is created that is linked to an association that the customer has. In the physical world this is how a customer relationship was built. The problem arises when the customer does not walk by the shop regularly, does not make many repeat purchases, such as in the electronics sector, or when the association with the shop is not positive. This can occur if the customer is disappointed in the purchase, has received poor treatment in the shop or has a different price perception. In order to convince customers, intensive and direct communication is necessary. This, however, is often lacking.

In the traditional buying process in the shop, the communication takes place through the shop and targeted advertising such as brochures and advertisements in the local media. There is often consultation between manufacturers and shopkeepers regarding the special offers, and the communication costs are shared. The shop is a leading party and the customer will be attracted to the shop because of these activities. In addition to this targeted communication, manufacturers will carry out their image promotions in order to positively influence the associations with the brand and to bring about a positive motivation among the customers. If, however, the shop does not have a good relationship with the manufacturer or if the manufacturer does not have a good relationship with the shopkeeper, conflicts will arise. The manufacturer would like to communicate directly with the customer, but this is tricky. Using the mass media the brand is built up and a general association with the product is created, but a targeted customer relationship is not possible. The battle for the customer is a battle for the customer ownership; with customer ownership, after all, you also have their contact details and you're able to maintain direct contact with them. Shopkeepers can ask for the contact details and ask customers for permission to communicate with them directly (via letters, telephone or email), but manufacturers have to come up with something different. In the 1990s this led to various brand-related clubs and activities.

These days all sorts of brand-related groups (communities) have been created on the Internet, particularly on social media sites such as Facebook and MySpace. This allows the manufacturer to communicate directly with customers (or fans) and stimulate the customers to buy their products or even refer them to shops where those products can be bought. With social media such as Facebook and MySpace this involves customer bonding and community building. For other social media such as YouTube this involves conveying brand values, whereas the main function of blogging sites such as Twitter is building direct relationships and communication. In all cases the relationships between the customer and the brand is supported.[5] As customers identify themselves with the brand, customer ownership arises, which enables direct communication. The more intensive the communication and the feeling of bonding, the more a customer buys in a conscious manner. Customer bonding is therefore of great importance to manufacturers and shops.

Collaboration has traditionally been a matter of sharing interests: direct communication and sales in the shop, brand associations and brand building using traditional media by the manufacturer. Joint direct activities aimed at individual customers. Due to the new buying behaviour, the use of the Internet and the possibility of coming into contact with customers in another way, a power struggle for the favour of the customer has arisen.

MIELE HAS HIGH EXPECTATIONS FROM DIRECT SALES

White goods manufacturer Miele is pulling out all the stops in order to reach the consumer. Through the Miele Inspirience Centre the manufacturer wants to discover the consumer's needs, and provides advice regarding their next purchase. Miele also expects to be able to

---

5   Increasingly more studies show that products can also be sold via Twitter. The tweets do, however, have to be targeted, up-to-date and not aggressive. Small companies can also benefit from this. See, for example, *5 Social Media Tips for Small Businesses* by Jeanne Hopkins, 7 June 2011, at blog.Hubspot.com.

*form a picture of the end user through the direct sales of accessories,
fittings and cleaning and maintenance materials. 'The fact that
these days increasingly more people approach the manufacturer for
information is something that you can clearly see,' says Robert Bakker,
Advertising and PR Manager.*

*Miele is not the only manufacturer that believes that direct contact with
the consumer is vitally important for the brand. This can be through an
attractively laid out showroom, an 'inspirience centre' and/or through
a webshop. Miele has chosen a broad strategy; since mid-April there has
been a brand-new webshop at Miele.nl. 'We had a webshop already,'
says Bakker, 'but we never gave it much publicity. The functionalities
of the new shop are far better.'*

*The company will never sell appliances directly to the consumer. 'We're
not looking to play a game of conquest,' says Bakker. 'Almost everyone
has a look around on the Internet, but in our sector the purchases are
often done offline. We sell through the chains, buying cooperatives,
wholesalers and the Internet. The consumer can choose himself which
channel to use to buy his products.'*

Source: Twinkle, 5 June 2009.

Which Purchase Choices Does a Custom Make at Home and Which in the Shop?

The reasons a customer looks for information on a particular product can vary
greatly. Perhaps it is due to a television commercial, or the simple desire to
buy something or in response to something the customer was told. Straight
to the Internet, a quick Google search and you're on your way. In this process
it does not make so much sense to go to your local shop. You first look up the
information on the Internet, and only then do you go to your preferred shop.
The shop that you choose can be one you already know, for example the shop
you have been advised by a comparison site or through a link on another site
(such as eBay). The bond with a webshop is often less strong than the one with
the physical shop. This is primarily due to the wide range of products on offer
and the limited top-of-mind position enjoyed by a webshop. Who knows where
he or she bought an electronic appliance the last time? The choice whether to
buy on the Internet or go to a shop is made in the living room. This is therefore

a crucial moment on which the shopkeeper has no influence. The shopkeeper now suddenly has to assume the role of a top-of-mind position or spontaneous loyalty of the customer, whereas the previous role was simply being *the* shop in the shopping street, relying on customer bonding through location.

A clear example of this is the book trade, where Internet sales have heralded difficult times for bookshops. There has been insufficient understanding of why customers buy books, and insufficient advantage is taken of the possibilities offered by the Internet. Webshops such as Amazon.com know their customers, communicate directly with an appropriate and personal product offer and also suggest books that are similar to the purchases that the customer has already made. As yet traditional retailers do not use this form of communication effectively. As in the case with Borders, the American bookshop chain, retailers do not know what form to give the shop to attract sufficient customers in order to make it profitable. Shelves and tables filled with products like books or clothes no longer seem to inspire these days. This typifies the current state of the retail sector.

It is all about the different role of shops and customers' different buying motives and considerations. The battle for the customer is therefore a battle for 'customer ownership', for the possibility of communicating directly with the customer. Loyalty and a top-of-mind position are built through recognition and a positive association. Communication helps in this. In this battleground the retailer still remains very much focused on old forms of communication, such as brochures and advertisements. Manufacturers also often still use mass communication. Webshops, however, make use of the new and direct forms of communication. This makes webshops a big threat for the traditional distribution channels and traditional shopkeepers in particular.

Battle for the Internet

Central to all of this is, of course, the customer. These days we can relax at home on the sofa with our laptop or tablet (iPad). We multitask, watching television, chatting with our partner, enjoying a glass of wine, while browsing the Internet. It can be fun to keep your Facebook page up-to-date or tweet your latest thoughts. The real breakthrough for home shopping came when wireless Internet also became possible at home. Its application developed steadily in parallel with that of laptops and netbooks (from 2006) and gained even further momentum thanks to the iPad. We were no longer buying on our immobile computer in the attic or in the bedroom, much to the relief of the respective partners who used to be left alone in the living room. We could now go on the Internet while still taking an active part in the family. The buying environment suddenly changed from a shop, to an attic room and finally to the living room. And one should not underestimate this effect. Buying on the Internet was something rational, if a little lonely on your own behind the computer. However, it has now become a social activity. *Social shopping* is now also possible at home.

DON'T DRINK AND CLICK, INTERNET SHOPPERS ARE WARNED ... AS DRUNK PURCHASES ARE USUALLY UNWANTED THE MORNING AFTER

- *Most drink-fuelled shopping is done between 11 p.m. and 1 a.m.*

- *One in seven admit they wouldn't have bought their drunk purchase.*

Almost half of Britons have shopped online after drinking, often falling asleep or having to abandon a transaction, new research showed today. Now consumers are being urged not to 'drink and click' after one in seven admitted buying something they never would when sober, with many sending it back immediately. More than half of online shoppers also spent more when tipsy – if they managed not fall asleep while purchasing. In a survey of more than 4,200 consumers, showed the most popular items bought online by 'boozy' shoppers were clothes and shoes, DVDs, books, video games, technology and lingerie. And although over half remembered shopping online the morning after, almost 20 per cent said they only realised they'd made the purchase the following day.

Source: *Daily Mail*, 7 December 2011.

The buying process nearly always starts at home. The great majority of people first look on the Internet before going to a shop to make an important purchase. This leads to customers becoming more forthright than in the past, and better informed prior to making the actual purchase. The buying process, looking around, research/information and communication takes place at home, whereas the action (buying) can take place both at home and in the shop. A dichotomy has emerged in the buying process and this is leading to a different type of buying behaviour, 'the new shopping '.

These days the customer first looks around on the Internet, while at home sat comfortably on the sofa. As soon as the purchase decision has been made it is decided where to buy the product; at home relaxing on the sofa, or in the shop. This buying decision moment is now at the home, but it used to be in the shop where a salesperson could give that final push towards a purchase.

If the retailer realises this he can take action. Such action would include aiming to achieve a top-of-mind position and building on loyalty more clearly. Some retailers introduced a customer card which took advantage of this change. For that reason it does not lend itself well to web shopping, as the buying behaviour of customers is different with this sort of item (this is then determined by the moment and impulse). In its efforts, however, to take advantage of this change, it uses personal communication through emails. This helps to give the customer relationship a central position and the direct communication leads to a top-of-mind position. Loyalty is built using (direct) communication. Even if the customer were to delete the email immediately, they would have already seen who sent it. This results in a combination of local presence, loyalty (the card) and direct communication (top-of-mind position).

The strength lies in the direct communication. Retailers can no longer continue to passively wait to see who comes into the shop, but must actively maintain a relationship with their customers. This requires customers wanting this relationship (opt-in), so that there is a customer ownership (via the opt-in). This can help to build up the customers' knowledge necessary for direct communication.

The Buying Conditions

At home people first look on the Internet. They weigh up the pros and cons after which they make the decision to buy. The conditions under which a decision to buy is taken has therefore changed. The traditional retailer can only play a limited role in this new buying decision, as can clearly be seen in the ORCA buying model. A customer's search structure (on the Internet) is often undetermined; but the closer he gets to the moment of purchase, the more prominent the retailer has to be (certainly in the thoughts of the customer). This can be done in various ways.

- by being present on the Internet with an online shop

- by being present on the Internet with an information site

- by creating affiliates on the Internet

- by modifying the shop

- through direct communication with customers

Of course, the retailer can set up its own online shop and in this way compete directly with the other Internet suppliers. The shop has name recognition amongst the customers and that in combination with the physical shop can provide considerable benefits. But on the Internet different rules apply, and the question is whether the retailer is aware of that. This will be examined in more detail in the next chapter.

A retailer would need at the very least an information site. This would help to position the shop on the Internet. This site should include location, photos of the shop, the opening hours, contact details and directions. The parking facilities and the product range sold should also be included in the basic information. The aim of this information site is to inform customers about the shop and to encourage them to visit it. The shop's contact details are important for allowing (potential) customers to contact the shop directly, by telephone, email or through a personal visit. Ensuring that the shop is also mentioned in all sorts of other sites, such as that of the local council, the shopping centre and the trade association, ensures it is found more quickly when someone is looking for a shop in the neighbourhood. What's more, other sites showing special deals also offer the possibility of logically referring visitors to the shop. This is important because the customer is in a buying process. If a customer is looking for a particular item then it is important for the item to be mentioned not only by the manufacturer, but also on trading sites such as eBay. Visitors search these sites for particular items. Sophisticated software often ensures that the products that are shown are those on offer within a particular action radius of the person logging in. Frequently these products are being offered by consumers themselves (peer-to-peer), and increasingly often we also see amongst them the products that are on sale in shops. These retailers can decide to advertise the shop in between all these products, often in a regular place or using a banner. A 'visitor' searches for a particular product, new or second-hand, and is immediately shown a local shop that also sells these products. As a result the visitor can consider whether or not to go to the shop for his purchase. A good salesman should then have a reasonable chance of making the sale. The combination of the Internet and the physical shop is a strong one.

All these factors have an influence on the moment of buying and the decision moment. For purchases that require more careful consideration this takes place at home, but the desire to have a look in the shop must be stimulated. The reasons a person would actually go to a shop are often personal; not wanting to wait for the product, uncertainty regarding the correctness of the purchase, loyalty to the shopkeeper or simply not being at home during the day. In all these cases the retail trade must be alert for the buyer who makes a conscious decision to go to the shop and who has already made up his mind. In addition, there are also those buyers who are still looking around, whereby the physical shop is part of this searching and buying process. These customers, too, are well-informed and want that 'final push' before buying the product. And finally, there is a third group. You can call this the impulse group, or perhaps the non-Internet group. In any case, they have not looked around on the Internet before going to the shop. That is not to say, however, that the Internet has no effect on the buying behaviour of this group whatsoever. This group is fully aware of the Internet, perhaps making use of it for other applications or being influenced by others who are active on the Internet. This group as a result is influenced in a secondary manner.

A Future for Shops?

The future of shops depends very much on what traditional shops do themselves to make shopping more fun and what shops do together to be attractive to customers. It is up to the shops to ensure that customers enjoy shopping by providing a good product range, decor, personnel and adding novel and exciting elements to the experience. In all cases buyers will make a conscious choice whereby the image, sales staff and the shop will play an important role. New shop concepts are based on the recreational character of shopping. Shopping is *fun* and should stay that way! In order to realise this, the decor of the shop has to contribute to this happy customer experience. This means being open and accessible, creating a clear form of freedom and making customers feel that they are important. The shops are there for the customers, not the other way round.

PROVEN SHOP CONCEPTS MUST TURN CARREFOUR PLANET INTO A SUCCESS

Carrefour recently opened its new concept shops in the Lyon region. The name: Carrefour Planet. The idea: not one large shop, but many different shop ideas under one roof. The French retail chain had conducted a survey among 60,000 households on how they prefer to do their shopping and came up with the Carrefour Planet. Hereby shop formulae of other retailers that had proven themselves in the past were largely duplicated. The new shop sets itself apart from the old shops in a number of important areas:

- *The cosmetics and beauty section is very much inspired by the French cosmetics chain Sephora. There is a nail and make-up service as well as a hairdressing salon.*

- *For the frozen food department the concept was inspired by the frozen food retail shops of Picard.*

- *There is a department for organic products whose layouts and product assortment very much resemble that of Bioplanet.*

- *The special furniture and household goods section strongly resembles IKEA.*

- *The fresh food department looks much like an old-fashioned fresh market.*

- *For electronics and media shop-in-shops were set up by partners Apple and Virgin.*

Perhaps the greatest step taken was the much more extensive service provision. For a small fee parents can drop their children off at a special play area, while they do their shopping at their leisure.

Source: Popai Benelux, 14 December 2010.

Responding to the wishes of customers is essential and perhaps even more important than product presentations. Women are given make-up sessions in the cosmetics department, there are reading corners in the book department, sometimes with cushions on the floor, and in the toy department there are children's play areas. Parents can see what their children enjoy playing with, and perhaps buy them afterwards. There is a coffee corner where biscuits and cakes are served, either to eat in or take home. These are just a few of the possibilities where entertainment is part of the shop concept. It may seem rather obvious to say, but if the sales staff are more interested in chatting with one another than with the customers, continue looking at the clock until it is lunch time, refuse a customer entrance five minutes before closing time or if they clearly do not enjoy what they are doing, why would a customer buy there at all? The shop staff have a major influence on the buying behaviour in the shop. They should be proud of working there, and this should be clear to the customer through their attitude and behaviour. Too often it is forgotten that sales staff are actually hosts and hostesses.

> *Top Shop is a British retailer that started in 1964 in Sheffield. It is a shop that sells inexpensive and fun clothes for young women. After Jane Shepherdson took charge of Top Shop in 1999 she introduced some major changes; not in the market position or the product range, but in the experience. The shop had to be exciting and unpredictable, and had to express a certain passion. She motivated the entire sales team to not so much follow the rules but to rely on their own feelings. Do what they think is best. The idea was simple: be there for you customers, forget the direct needs of the business. Ensure there is a good and pleasant buying experience.*
>
> *Source*: Richard Hammond, *Smart Retail*, 3rd edition, 2011, Harlow: Pearson Education, p. 51.

Hospitality

In Japan I was regularly greeted by a salesperson in the shop with the words 'Welcome to my shop', along with the customary bowing. That certainly made me feel welcome! I had the same feeling in America when I spoke to the sales staff of small shops. They appeared genuinely pleased at my arrival and did their very best to help me. This also involved showing me other products that I could buy (with a discount that was only for me!). The most striking example was in Watering Tower in Chicago where the saleswoman kept on showing me other matching products that I could get with a discount. This made me so happy that I kept on buying products there, and eventually was given a gift on my departure. It was, of course, a sales ploy, but the personal touch, the feeling that this was only for me and that I was given personal advice, made me happy and eager to buy! Unfortunately, you don't get this feeling in all countries. Often the sales staff will serve you out of an obligation to carry out the transaction. Pay quickly and off you go! If shops forget that customers are people with human feelings, then they are only appealing to our rational mind, and our rational mind can always be better directed towards the Internet. So in order to combat the Internet, shops should not compete on the basis of rational considerations and price, but on the basis of other *value drivers* that can differ from customer to customer. Realise this and put it into practice!

Collaboration/Affiliates

But shops also have to collaborate to attract customers. An effective way of doing this is for the shop to be part of a total concept. This is the case with the Trafford Centre in Manchester, as well with shops located alongside the local football stadium in a shopping centre or in a city centre. In all these cases the concept has to be attractive enough to appeal to shops. In the Dutch town of Beverwijk they are working on a new shopping experience using the appeal of its famous 'black market'. By connecting this with the city centre, using a new pedestrian route and the integration of catering facilities such as bars and restaurants, visitors of the 'black market' are automatically guided towards the centre.

A similar initiative also led to *Sportstad Heerenveen* in the city of Heerenveen in the Netherlands. This is a concentration of sports facilities, in the centre of which is the football stadium and probably soon also the ice skating rink Thialf. This will help to draw a large public into Heerenveen. *Sportstad Heerenveen* is within walking distance of the city centre. The shops will be able to benefit from the appeal of the sports centre by attracting visitors and customers outside the city's usual buying zone. In these cases the old city centre is still being used as a shopping centre, but is made more attractive by capitalising on other nearby activities such as the 'black market' or sports facilities. However, this is by no means always the case, leading to old city centres no longer being regarded as appealing shopping centres. And it is often made worse by a restrictive policy regarding parking and accessibility. It sometimes seems as if customers are being chased away by the policies of the local councils. And so the solution is sought in out-of-town shopping centres located on the outskirts of the city. These shopping centres provide recreational facilities such as cinemas, casinos, discos and of course plenty of parking facilities. The strength of the appeal is a mix of factors, but the core element is simple: how can you respond to the wishes of customers? These centres often have long opening hours, and are open in the evenings and on Sundays. The customer then determines whether shopping at those times meets a particular need.

Service and Out-of-Town Shopping Centre

A few years ago trials were carried out with *non-stop shopping* in supermarkets in the week leading up to Christmas. Research had shown that customers felt frustrated with the long queues at the checkouts. *Non-stop shopping* made it possible for customers to go to the supermarkets in the evenings and at night. This, however, was not a resounding success. The solution for the long queues at the checkouts was found in home deliveries (and paying with your customer card) as well as scanning your items yourself. The queues at the checkouts are now significantly shorter, also during the week before Christmas, and the shops are closed again between 10 in the evening and 6 in the morning.

These new shopping centres are often not located in the centre of the city and this as a result will lead to changes to the city centre. Manchester is a good example, where the Trafford Centre has led to reduced numbers of shoppers in the centre, more empty properties of former shops and a change in the products being sold. On the other hand, the housing function of the city centres has increased, which occurred hand-in-hand with the emergence of smaller shops and catering facilities such as bars and restaurants. The Saturday crowds have made way for a more evenly spread visit to the centre, but of course the number of visitors is much lower than it was before. Even the large department stores have opened more smaller shops in the centre. The large shops are now based in the Trafford Centre, whilst it is also possible to buy on the Internet (*click and collect!*). This development can be seen in other cities as well where large shopping centres have been located outside the city centre. It may appear a threat for the existing shops in the centre but that does not have to be. The shopping centre acts as a large magnet whereby visitors from far afield are attracted to the local area. As a result the city centre can change into a residential, cultural and catering centre with its own unique public with its own particular wishes. It will be a transformation to a place with good restaurants and cafes and a good nightlife. A place with culture, entertainment, small boutiques, and specialised shops is the future of a city centre. Of course the city centres will be smaller, shops will be more concentrated but therefore also better to reach for customers. No long walks after parking the car and no sky-high parking fees either. If a city is able to transform into a leisure place with shops that surprise in a cultural setting with entertainment it has a new future. Going back to the old days with supermarkets in town has no real sense. That makes the city a pleasant place to live, where you go out for meals and drinks, or to the theatre. And in turn it offers opportunities to smaller shops, specialty shops and boutiques. It gives the city centre a unique and distinctive character. This *out-of-town shopping centre* is the magnet for the entire region, and the city has to adapt to this new role. This situation creates room for smaller shops, specialty and creative shops and boutiques, along with cafes, restaurants and bars. It is a development that responds not only to the wishes of the customer, who wants more enhanced experiences, other forms of recreation and leisure, but also to the new buying behaviour. Shops will only survive this development if they have a clear vision of the future, if there is the will to respond to the new buying behaviour and the wishes of the customers, and if retailers realise that the new retail landscape is different from the present one.

Changes are Opportunities and Threats

Customers have choices due to the increased mobility, larger living and economic environments (the home and place of work are often located far from one another) and the adoption of the Internet. As a result they place other demands on the shop. What's more, in the coming years the ageing population will lead to a shift in the ownership of the smaller shops. Many owners will reach retirement age and will wish to sell their shop. If there is no buyer, the shop will have to close. If there is a buyer, however, it will be a young and dynamic one. The shop will change and as a result will immediately bring about a change in the buying public. All in all, an uncertain future for shops. The Internet will be a dominant factor within the retail sector, as will be clear in the following chapter. The real solution, however, lies in optimising the individual strengths of physical shops and motivating customers to visit them. Chapter 4 will show that this requires insight, empathy and creative thinking, key elements to the future of retail. Shops must be inspiring, surprising and welcoming places to visit. They have to possess expert knowledge, inspire trust and provide service. Only then is there a future!

> In 2007 Primark, a real no-nonsense business for low-priced clothes, opened a flagstore in Oxford Street, London. This was immediately a gigantic success: on the opening day the queues even extended to outside the shop. The number of visitors on that first day was estimated at tens of thousands. The buying public of Primark is the same as the public

that shops at Selfridges, Debenhams, John Lewis Next and Gap, all high street shops. By offering low prices customers are given the feeling that they have something extra, that they have beaten 'the system'. After all, everyone loves a bargain in this bargain-driven culture. An amusing fact is that the Primark carrier bags are almost always thrown away outside the shop, and the purchased item put into other bags. You should be able to boast about a bargain, but not to everyone.

Source: Richard Hammond, *Smart Retail*, 3rd edition, 2011, Harlow: Pearson Education, p. 117.

Conclusion and Summary of Chapter 3

The retailer has to fight on various fronts, but these days increasingly also in a different manner. There are opportunities to win each battle but then the retailer would have to be flexible and very much focused on customers' wishes and needs. Direct communication will be an important weapon.

Table 3.2   Conclusion and summary

Pressure on retail	Due to	Opportunities	Trend
New buying behaviour.	Social changes, social demography, freedom of choice, shopping = recreating.	New concepts, services, experience and surprises. Motivate customers to visit.	Internet is becoming a major sales channel, breakthrough of mobile Internet services.
Internet.	Information, communication and buying medium, social media.	Interest in websites, communicate directly, active on social media.	Mobile Internet, location-based services. Always be connected.
Suppliers.	Direct communication, *flagstores*, direct supply.	Develop concepts, *partnership*, collaboration.	Collaboration with major retailers, owned shops and the Internet.
Transparency.	Pressure on the margins, substitutes.	Customisation is difficult to compare, services as extra component, personal advice.	Low-priced guarantees. Daily special offers, *flash stores*.
Traditional profit maker.	Property decline, pressure on margins and on *trade margins*.	Develop new concepts, new profit makers.	Margin on products is increasingly coming under pressure; there is, however, still a margin on services.
Continuity.	Problems with succession, customer loyalty and supplies.	Collaboration, *affiliate*.	Remains a major problem in the future.

4

Webshops: The Future for Retail? The Grass Is Always Greener on the Other Side

The Threat Posed by the Internet

It seems all so easy. Just apply for a domain name, make a website and there you have it – your own shop on the Internet. You have no other costs such as for shop premises, warehouse, staff or advertising costs. You could even start your business from your bedroom. The many webshops are looked upon with jealousy by retailers, who have to find a good location, rent or buy their business premises, lay out the shop and advertise. Webshops certainly seem to have it easy. Unfair competition as far as retailers are concerned, which is often confirmed by the competitive prices. What's more, customers are also increasingly buying ever more products on the Internet. The growth percentages for the coming years are estimated at between 10% and 15% each year, making a possible turnover of *15 billion* in 2015 a very realistic figure (approximately 30% of non-food retail). And this turnover will, of course, be at the expense of the turnover of the existing retail trade. This certainly makes the Internet a real threat to the existing retail trade, and so the feeling of unfair competition is understandable. Webshops do not require any licence to establish a business, have no restrictive opening hours, have no parking problems, require limited investments and, what's more, they can benefit from the economic tide propelled by the new buying behaviour. But do existing retailers focus too much on the advantages of webshops and not on the disadvantages? Is it possible that here, too, the grass is greener on the other side of the fence?

According to recent statistics, we did 13.5% of our shopping online in 2010 and according to BCG that is expected to rise to as much as 26% by 2016. If you run a small-medium sized business this figure may concern you, especially if you rely entirely on one-to-one contact with your customers – but it shouldn't. In the UK, Online shopping makes up 8.3% of the total economy - the biggest share of all the G20 countries. That's a share which is bigger than the healthcare, construction or education sectors.

Source: Dave Burton, doivedesigns.co.uk, 21 March 2012.

With physical products shops have a great advantage over the Internet, as these products have to be either delivered to the customers (by the webshop) or collected from the shop by the customer. The shop, therefore, has two important roles for these products: a distribution role and an advisory role. With virtual products, however, it is the webshops that have an advantage, as no delivery to the house is necessary. Customers can after all buy and download the products directly from the Internet. This is also the reason that travel agencies, music shops and bookshops are slowly disappearing from the high street. As these products are virtual, they can be downloaded by customers. It is therefore no longer necessary to go to the shop.

The Development of the Internet

The Internet had its origins as a message service, a sort of bulletin board where everyone could leave behind messages for others to read. This bulletin board function is still visible in the various social media websites such as the wall on Facebook, where people can respond to one another's messages. Here, however, you have to actively find out what is being said, so the development from a bulletin board to a communication platform is a logical step. Email was quickly a *killer app*. Both of these applications were simple, as not a great deal of (technical) knowledge was required. Websites that provided information emerged quickly and later on also online shops. The further development of the Internet took place along these four parallel lines: communication applications, information applications, purchase/trade applications and finally infrastructural applications. We also see these four applications, in sequence, in the adoption by customers. Internet users normally have a mailbox of their service provider or use a free mailbox, for example Gmail or Hotmail. They surf on the net and search for information. When searching and surfing, a search engine such as Bing or Google is usually used. These search engines are very user-friendly and even correct typing and spelling mistakes.

The biggest step that an Internet user takes is when he buys on the net. People can feel a little unsure when buying and paying on the Internet. One's own personal experience (or lack thereof) can play a role in this, as well as concerns about whether the company or supplier is well known, or about the payment methods used (payment in advance or payable in arrear), or a home-shopping guarantee hallmark, the price or perhaps even personal motives. After a few cautious initial purchases, such as books or a purchase from a well-known (physical) shop, the trust grows along with the use of the Internet as a buying option. The following step in the development and use of the Internet is an integral platform. The users are therefore always accessible with a smartphone, tablet or a computer. The Internet is a 'facilitator' of services such as telephony, navigation, location-based services and, of course, social media. Once the Internet is fully accepted and widely used there will be a further convergence in its use, whereby all functions can be integrated. The user would then no longer be consciously aware of the Internet being used, as the application would be central to all activities. This development is now fully underway with, for example, Wi-Fi. Being online is possible everywhere and at all times. Increasing numbers of companies and shopping centres are offering free Wi-Fi connections, allowing all Internet facilities to be used whilst you are shopping, dining or travelling. It is on these mobile applications and convergence that the new developments in the use of the Internet are being based. Chapters 6 and 7 will examine these in more detail.

Buying on the Internet: From the Perspective of the Product

Customers are embracing the Internet as a new retail channel. In 90% of purchases that require some degree of consideration, the customer first looks on the Internet before buying the product. The buying model (ORCA) shows that Google (or Bing) is the first entry point, but that the customer then soon after visits a product site or online shop. At home on the sofa the buying resistance is low. The atmosphere is good and you feel happy, and so buying just adds to this feeling. If you can buy straightaway, why wait? Going to the shop requires some extra effort, which may not even be necessary. For virtual products it is no longer logical to go to the shop. Due to certain products shifting from physical to virtual formats, as is the case with music, software, news (newspapers, magazines) and now also books, the old distribution channel, through shops, is under a great deal of pressure. A consequence of this change has been the large-scale reorganisation of music shops and book stores. For retailers of physical products the Internet has not had such a great impact, but that is just a matter of time. Increasingly more facilities are becoming available and ordering online is often an option, whereby if you order the product on the day by a certain time it will be delivered to your door the following day. Many postal organisations now recognise the opportunities open for providing an efficient delivery of ordered products and so are developing their business models accordingly. The time someone has to wait to receive ordered items is therefore becoming shorter.

THE PRODUCTS OFFERED ON THE INTERNET

The first physical products that were offered were convenient, risk-free products for the buyer, such as books and CDs: cheap, simple and easy to deliver. The buyers did not run any real risks, certainly when paying on delivery. These are known products that require some degree of consideration before purchase, such as music and books. Not a great deal of support was necessary for making these purchases. For the suppliers, apart from a website not many modifications were necessary. Books were already stored in a central distribution centre, which delivered to the book dealers on behalf of the publishers. And the music industry was already being protected by copyright. No extra modifications were necessary to the infrastructure and the website could be kept relatively simple. Anyone could set up a webshop quickly, and customers actually had no barriers in their way to buying there. It was relatively simple for new customers to get accustomed to home shopping.

Airline companies have, perhaps unintentionally, given a tremendous boost to the use of the Internet. Budget airlines such as EasyJet and Ryanair looked for ways to reduce their costs and to compete with the established airlines through cheap tickets. The Internet turned out to be a good instrument for keeping down costs. Customers could book their flights directly themselves and pay in advance, and due to the direct link between the booking system and the reservation system no human intervention was required. What's more, no commission had to be paid to booking agents. Particularly the older generation who wanted to use these budget airlines for attractive destinations in southern Europe started to book directly, and so became accustomed to the Internet and buying online. This turned out to be a breakthrough for virtual products. However, it was also immediately an acceptance of the Internet as an important purchasing channel.

After books and CDs came the virtual products such as holidays, airline tickets and software. These suppliers first had to carry out some adjustments to the technical platform before it was possible to book the products. Software had to be downloaded and a different type of payment system had to be introduced. Sometimes security also had to be incorporated within the system. For airline tickets a link to the reservation and booking system was necessary, and then later other systems for boarding and seating reservations. These virtual products have the great advantage that there are no physical restrictions, no costs per product and no delivery charges. This led to these particular virtual products being regarded as a possible profit machine. Once the system had been set up products could be sold on the Internet without any additional costs. It was therefore quite understandable that suppliers went searching for this type of product; from games to software, from virus scanners to news subscriptions or access to sites. Particularly the pornography industry was the great pacesetter, as access to a site did not require payment, the product had no language barriers and it appealed to a large group of potential (international) customers. As the number of visitors increased no extra costs were incurred; so every new visitor was immediate profit. Money was, and still is, earned through banners and click-through options.

After the virtual products and due to the increase in Internet use, growing numbers of new suppliers recognised the opportunities offered by the Internet as a channel for buying. Existing mail-order companies saw the Internet as an efficient replacement of the catalogue, whilst the banks recognised that the Internet would allow a more efficient way of processing payment orders. These were logical entrants to the Internet who offered Internet facilities to customers as an extra service without having to make any changes to their own proposition. Although online ordering through mail-order companies and online banking through banks were actually offered as services, they ended up leading to large cost savings in processing the orders. This was very much a double-edged sword. The benefits for the banks were even greater as customers were prepared to pay extra for Internet banking, whilst in reality this actually saved the banks costs (!). After these logical entrants, new entrants emerged who began to sell products that perhaps were not available locally or products that the customer wanted to buy on the Internet: special products, collector's items, special wines and diet products that were not normally sold in local shops. Others suppliers saw the possibility of increasing their market reach.

The development is very much in full swing, with increasingly more companies wanting to supply products on the Internet convinced of the considerable opportunities. It is this larger market reach and the relatively simple manner in which products can be sold on a website that is so appealing.

The problem arises only later (as will be explained further on in this chapter). Due to the ever-increasing growth of products available on the Internet and the increasing number of users, the Internet is becoming ever more important as a distribution channel and buying medium. But supply also needs a demand, customers have to want to buy on the Internet; acceptance and trust are therefore necessary.

VIRTUAL PRODUCTS ARE IDEAL FOR THE INTERNET

Virtual products have the advantage that no waiting time is required for the delivery; buying and receiving the product take place almost simultaneously. This is a considerable advantage, making the Internet an ideal medium for supplying virtual products. And it is the reason that the music world has changed so much in such a short time. It is after all far easier to download music than to go to a shop to buy a CD. A similar development occurred with software and airline tickets. Airline companies such as Ryanair and Transavia sell their tickets only through the Internet. In fact their entire business model is based on the Internet. Their customers book the journey on the Internet where they can even print out their boarding pass. In view of the great advantages of virtual products, such as free distribution and the fact that they are multipliable without costs, increasingly more products are being produced in virtual form. Reports, films and television programmes are clear examples of this. In some cases, however, a form of infrastructure is necessary; a good device in order to be able to use these (virtual) products effectively. For music this was the mp3 player. The mp3 player became a popular replacement of the old Walkman (based on cassette tapes), and so an infrastructure necessary for downloading music emerged naturally. Apple in particular played a major role in this. The iPod initially became popular due to its modern design, and then later it was supported by iTunes. By using iTunes it was possible to download the music on the iPod, whilst at the same time ensuring that music copyrights were properly paid for. And so this tackled the old problem of illegal downloading. And as it was also possible to download single music tracks (at low costs), the combination of iPod and iTunes quickly became a success.

The same methodology was used with the introduction of the iPad. With the acceptance of the iPad as a new mobile computer, a platform was created for new possibilities, the 'apps'. This involves installing software that enables a particular type of application. By paying for the 'app' (supplier or user) it was possible to ask for money for virtual products, but it was also possible to make physical products virtual. The online newspapers are clear examples of this, where virtual newspapers are under threat of being replaced by physical ones. This has resulted in a conflict between the physical and virtual world, where publishers have to take a fresh look at their future and business model. And it is the users that determine whether they want this or not, how they want it and what this will mean for publishers.

A similar sort of replacement from physical to virtual is taking place with books. Thanks to the introduction of eReaders it is possible to produce virtual books. Books can now be downloaded and no longer have to be printed in definite print runs. It is therefore possible to sell large quantities without incurring extra costs. The e-book reader so far has not been that popular, but the breakthrough may come in the application of the increasingly popular iPad and tablets. Users would then no longer require a specific *reader* but would use the necessary 'app' on the tablet. The sale of e-books, of course, takes place online. It will also make sense to see a convergence of *devices*. After all, you would not want to lug various devices around with you such as a smartphone, tablet, laptop and perhaps even an e-book reader. The ease of use plays a major role in the users accepting the medium and therefore also the further development of the Internet. This development and its impact on retail will receive particular attention in Chapter 5.

Buying on the Internet: From the Perspective of the Customer

Buying on the Internet starts with the customer searching. A customer searches using various criteria, such as company name, product name, brand or (other) search terms. It is important to know which of these criteria are used. Suggestions are continually given and in this way a customer surfs on the Internet, often from site to site. If a website appeals to the surfer straightaway it is examined further. This is why the first page is so important in tempting the visitor to take a closer look at the site. Women in particular tend to hop from site to site less than men, but prefer to examine a particular site more closely (women on average view four times as many pages as men). With all this web surfing, customers are not able to keep track of the sites they have visited, and often cannot recall from where they bought a particular product. In addition, only negative experiences tend to be remembered, and positive ones just taken for granted. During the search a shortlist is made (in one's mind) which the surfer uses for a comparison. Based on a shortlist, often at product level, it is decided what is the best product and where best to buy it. Comparison websites play an important part in this process. Linking the comparison site to other websites creates traffic to these particular websites.

GOOGLE TAKES THE PRICE COMPARISON MARKET
BY STORM

With the arrival of the new price comparison website Google Shopping the traditional comparison sites such as kelkoo.co.uk, pricerunner. co.uk, shopping.com and moneysavingexpert.com will have to contend with a formidable competitor.

The 'regular' price comparison websites each reach about 10% of the Internet uses, whereas Google could reach up to the 90% mark in the Netherlands. The consumer no longer has to go to different sites, but can do this with a single search engine. What's more, Google Shopping has the extra benefit that the reviews of the products offered come largely from the Dutch consumer association, the Consumentenbond. They therefore come across as more reliable than reviews from a random Internet user.

In every country where Google Shopping – also called Google Product Search – has been introduced up to now, the existing price comparisons have had to face the consequences. 'In France, for example, we have seen Google acquire a considerable search volume in just a short period of time,' says Uriel Ballast, director of shop2market, a company that helps webshops present themselves on the Internet 'It has not quite been a demolition, but the home, garden and kitchen comparison sites have received significantly fewer clicks. They have had to modify their websites and for example add more information and videos. We will notice this here as well.' Google Shopping offers shops that want to display their products on the Internet not only a wider reach but also another particular benefit. They do not have to pay any costs in order to be mentioned on Google. Currently webshops have to pay between 10 to 15 euro cents if a customer responds to an offer via a price overview.

However, with Google it won't continue to be 'free' for long, assures Ballast. Once Google manages to attract and retain many webshops, it will become increasingly difficult to stand out amongst the enormous numbers of products on offer. 'In order to get higher up on the list, one will soon turn to paid services.'

The fact that Google has called in the Consumentenbond, the Dutch consumer association, is a good development according to Ballast. 'Reviews are always good, even negative ones. This helps to create trust.' For the time being reviews from the Consumentenbond are confined to six product groups: washing machines, dishwashers, digital cameras, vacuum cleaners, mobile phones and televisions.

Source: www.BNdestem.nl.

This search process eventually leads to a webshop, but not just like that. There has to be a top-of-mind position or a link from another site (an affiliate). This is possible by ensuring that the product in question is listed as a search term (tag) on the site and that the design takes into account this association (link), whereby it would be listed in a search engine such as Bing or Google.

ATTRACTING VISITORS

Another way of getting visitors to the website is banners alongside the products, links on the product site or using price comparison sites. In all cases there has to be a link between the product and the shop. It is also possible to insert a link on the classified ads sites. If someone then searches for a particular product on the website of relevant shops in the neighbourhood will therefore be mentioned as well; this could be done either in a regular place on a list of results or in the form of an advertisement. A top-of-mind link of a product with a shop is much more difficult; shops sell many different products and brands and so what sort of association does a customer make? This (un)linking between products and shops, both when searching and in the top of the mind of some customers, can lead to product and brand manufacturers making their own websites where they can insert direct links to the retailers (the sales channel) or sell their products directly themselves. Through this link the manufacturers show some respect for the channel and recognises the benefits a retailer can add to the buying process. In some cases manufacturers also make a distinction between the type of shops (specialist or general, with or without service). Based on the postcode (or the login point) the relevant shops in the neighbourhood can be displayed. For the customer this is an extra service, certainly if they also require more information about the shop, such as online purchasing possibilities, opening hours or the stock level of the product in question.

The methodology for referral is called 'affiliate marketing' and is an important part of e-marketing. With 'affiliate marketing' a website is chosen that will refer to a webshop. One party, the one that is able to attract customers, is the affiliate and the other party is the classified ads site that wishes to sell a product. In this way, traffic is created for a webshop, which can also immediately analyse where the traffic came from, from which affiliates, and whether the visit is spontaneous or originated from a search engine. In itself it can be quite a challenge for webshops to find the right affiliate that generates traffic to their site, exudes the right look and feel for customers and charges a reasonable amount per lead.

SEARCHING FOR INFORMATION

For the customer it is important that sufficient information is offered: during the orientation process to be able to make a selection, during the information process to be able to compare products and during the buying process to be able to make a sound decision regarding whether to buy online or offline and from which physical retailer or webshop. Subjective elements often play a role in this process such as familiarity with the site or product, the general feeling created by the site, speed at replying to emails, messages posted on social media sites as well as simply your mood at the time. From the perspective of a buyer it is important that the entire process of orientation, information, communication and buying is supported well. If this all can take place on the same website of a single supplier, then this has benefits for both the customer and the supplier. Customers can receive better assistance and gain trust in the website on the one hand, and suppliers are better able to analyse what happens 'on-site' and so improve their website and respond more effectively to the customers' individual needs and wishes on the other. A direct link to the supporting websites is a good solution. As a result, the customer may think he is still on the supplier's site, but in fact has been linked to another supplier regarding this particular component. Close corporation between the various parties and a good integration of the link (*embedded software*) is necessary for this. This solution is chosen in order to have a direct link with a comparison site or supplier (in the *supply chain*). The webshops can help with good objective product information, delivery information and guaranteeing the delivery with for example a home-shopping guarantee hallmark. Customers should not get the feeling that they are being sold something. Rather, they should feel that they themselves are buying something. This is an essential difference for customers.

BUYING

For customers the main difference between webshops and physical shops is the way in which products are bought. With physical shops women tend to go into the town centre and into those shops that appeal to them. They browse and look around, buying the occasional item. Often a shop is chosen and a product bought that appeals to the customer or simply makes her feel happy. The shopping behaviour displayed by men in physical shops is very different. Men often intentionally go back to the same shop as this has become their preferred place to go shopping. They quickly buy something and leave again. They don't want to waste their time shopping, though an exception is made when it comes to electronics. Men certainly do like technology (and sports). When buying electronic equipment they tend to spend a great deal of time looking at the products and comparing them extensively. A shop like MediaMarkt takes advantage of this by making shopping an experience. A wide range of a great many products, apparent low prices and plenty of demonstrations. One is allowed to touch the products, and a salesperson is always near at hand to further accentuate that happy feeling, looking for information, seeing and wanting, all at the same time. Women don't have this feeling with electronics and therefore buy on more rational grounds, often also on the basis of design. And this is why women tend to buy electronics on the Internet more often than men. For clothing this is precisely the opposite, for the reasons given above.

A major change in the buying behaviour is also the relationship with, or preference for, a particular shop a customer may have. With the traditional buying behaviour there was a strong association with a shop and the product range offered at the shop. In some cases the bond was so strong that a product would be bought regardless of the brand. These days there is greater brand awareness, customers show less loyalty towards shops and the options available to customers are much greater (more brands, more products and more shops through the Internet). The bonding of a customer has shifted from a bond with a (local) shop to one with a product (brand). Also the social changes as described in Chapter 1, whereby people prefer to be more identified with groups and imitate the group behaviour, have an influence on the buying behaviour and the choice of brand.

SHOP BONDING DECREASES WHILST PRODUCT BONDING IS ON THE RISE

Brands are increasingly looking to fit in with this group behaviour and the group identification. As a result brands can be the binding factor of a group. This leads to an increasing brand preference (with group identification) and a decreasing preference for shops. The Internet stimulates this change as people tend to search on the basis of products or brands. A well-known brand instils more trust in the correctness of the purchase, greatly exceeding the trust people have in shops. Shops, however, have to ensure that they do not compromise this brand trust if they also sell this particular brand. The split purchase decision between a product/brand and choosing where to buy it reveals a breakdown of this buying behaviour. Customers tend to buy articles separately and make a separate purchase decision for each article, per product and per (web)shop.

Travel agents sell packages and all-in holidays, whilst on the Internet the products are sold separately: a hotel or holiday park, the necessary flight and perhaps also a rental car. Quite often the type of holiday is chosen first along with the location, and only then are the supporting products such as airline tickets, hotel or rental car bought. Customers have become more forthright, as they now have a total overview thanks to the Internet. They can arrange everything themselves. It is only when customers are very uncertain or do not want too much bother that they choose a total package through a travel agency, either offline or online. Webshops have to be aware of this new buying behaviour and not simply imitate the physical shops, as buying on the Internet is also a question of convenience and trust.

Another challenge for selling on the Internet is the element of originality. Many websites are boring and too clinical, simply showing a total overview of products, all neatly arranged. This does not appeal to the emotions but to the rational mind. Associated products are often not offered either, such as shoes to go with a dress or a jacket with a matching shawl. Men, being fairly lazy buyers in general, prefer to buy a total concept; a shirt for example with matching tie and cufflinks. No endless searching and no risks, and afterwards this combination often continues to be worn together. The challenge for webshops is not only to offer products that appeal to the rational side of customers but also to take advantage of this association or to surprise the customer. And it is this in turn that provides hope for the real shops.

Opportunities for Webshops

The opportunities for webshops lie firstly in the weaknesses of the existing shops and consequently also in the new shopping behaviour of buyers. The existing shops are faced with the problem of physical presence and physical restrictions.

The weaknesses of the physical shops are in turn the opportunities for webshops. And if webshops take advantage of them then they will, of course, immediately emphasise those weaknesses of the physical shops. And on top of

Table 4.1   Problems of physical shops compared to webshops

Physical shop	Webshop
Physical location, limited reach	Internet is worldwide, thereby giving room for specialisation
Limited product range	Unlimited product range possible
Limited opening hours	24/7
No knowledge of individual customers	A great deal of knowledge of individual customers
No direct communication	Only direct communication
Physical shopping costs time (during the day)	Efficient, rational, as well as in the evenings

this there are many more advantages open to webshops due to the application of the latest technology.

AREAS OF ATTENTION FOR WEBSHOPS

Name

It is however not that easy for webshops to take advantage of these opportunities. When setting up a webshop it is first of all necessary to have a good name; one that is distinctive and can communicate the purpose immediately. In addition, the site must have the right look and feel, must be easy to navigate and appeal to the intended target group. It has to be easy to buy on the website and the visitors have to be assisted in buying (more) through, for example, offering alternatives or showing what other visitors have already bought. The Internet is a very competitive medium, where customers are able to quickly compare many different offers and sites with one another. It is a worldwide network of countless suppliers. Webshops therefore really have to do their best to stand out.

The Internet is also a network which allows suppliers to enter the market quickly and without any real restrictions. Just apply for a domain name, set up a website and then you're ready; you now have a business. This all requires little costs and effort; worldwide there are some 850 million websites in operation. These are primarily companies with a .com extension, but many other countries also have their own extensions such as .nl for the Netherlands, .fr for France and .co.uk for the UK. There are some eccentric names around, which have been thought up without much consideration for whether customers would be able to remember them, let alone spell them. Businesses too often tend to stick to their company name instead of an object name or a name that is based on their objectives, such as shirts.com and charities.com.

The domain name must make sense to the customer, must be easy to spell, easy to remember and also, of course, still available. Too often the mistake is made of choosing a domain name that the supplier considers logical, but which is not necessarily so to their customers. Company names or particular fancy names that may work well in the physical world do not always succeed in the world of the Internet. Webshop owners particularly have to avoid the possibility of spelling mistakes. These names may work well in the physical world, whereby the location or the person is important but on the Internet this name has to be searched for. The customer has to be able to remember the name, and on the Internet the chance of typing mistakes must be kept to a minimum. For strong companies and strong brands the company name may well work effectively; however, if the name is not so well known to the Internet visitor then it would be better to use a fictitious name. Existing retailers rely on the fact that they are strong brands and well known, so also require no further explanation. But for most of the other suppliers, however, this is necessary.

Attract Visitors

Webshops have to be aware of the reasons for customers visiting their website and wanting to buy. Often the customer first has to get to the website in question by clicking on a particular link, which can be seen through, for example, *Google alerts*. A good strategy based on the search and surfing behaviour is therefore necessary to attract customers. Once the visitor is on the website the business has to respond as effectively as possible to the wishes of this visitor, taking into account the conscious and subconscious uncertainties. A good search structure, clear payment possibilities and also perhaps a home-shopping guarantee hallmark provides confidence and trust. A prominent contact button also helps, because a customer would want to know who owns the site and where to go if they require further assistance, have any complaints or need to contact someone for other reasons. Effective websites are characterised by their orderliness, good *look and feel* and trust that they exude through their layout, colour and navigation. Shops have the great advantage that they have direct contact with the visitor.

The behaviour of the visitor can be seen and monitored, allowing the search process to be optimised and enabling the webshop to respond to the customers' wishes more effectively. Particularly the possibility of behavioural targeting is interesting, whereby online suggestions can be carried out on the basis of the observed search behaviour. It is also possible to provide these suggestions if the same visitor returns within a few days. Customers after all can be recognised from their IP number or login code. Through this recognition the affinity with a certain webshop increases, although there are other ways of doing this, such as newsletters, customised special offers and suggestions. For the webshop it is important to gain the customer's attention in order to acquire a top-of-the-line position. With physical shops, potential customers constantly walk by. It is possible to make eye contact and thereby prompt an automatic top-of-mind position. This doesn't happen on the Internet; you don't just come across a website; it is always a conscious decision. We therefore have to build up a top-of-mind position using communication, constantly trying to attract the (potential) customer's attention. A newsletter, for which the customers have registered through an opt-in, is one such way, providing this is sent frequently (for example every two weeks). Even if customers do not open the email, they do still see the name of the webshop. If the customer does not opt out from receiving the email then he either attaches some value to it or simply cannot be bothered; either way it really does not matter. For webshops the direct communication is very important. This direct communication must be frequent and aimed at the behaviour of the customer or his expectations. It is often better not to make too many special offers with products. It is usually better to simply provide information. This helps you to arrive at a buying process earlier, which gives you a better position if something has to be bought. Fashion companies, for example, can send monthly fashion news, targeted to the preferred brands or style of the customer as much as possible. Sports companies can send news about those sports in which customers have expressed an interest or on the basis of items that have been bought in the past. So if a customer has bought, for example, football boots it would be a good idea to send monthly news on football, or if a customer has bought cycling clothes in the past then a monthly newsletter on cycling would be appropriate. This helps to create a high attention value for the recipient. It is also possible to look for affiliates based on these interests, such as acquiring links on football sites that refer potential customers to football equipment on your own website. As the newsletters have some value as a source of news, this increases the attention value. The result is an increased association with the webshop.

Communication

Another important point of attention is the speed at which questions and requests for contacts are responded to. The webshop has the advantage of being open all the time, but the support provided by its staff, of course, cannot be available every hour of the day. On the basis of the visitor behaviour it can be decided to open the customer service department at times when many visitors may be expected. This may be after a newsletter or television advertisement, or simply at peak times, often in the evenings. As service provided by email, chat or telephone may be sufficient for this, it is not necessary to be in the office. You can easily access your mailbox from home where you can answer any queries. At home you can also be reached by telephone (with calls being transferred from the office), or you can chat on the computer from home, with or without a webcam. This allows support to be given at those times that the customers are active; after all, the customers should be allowed to indicate the best time for support to be available. Of course, this doesn't have to be all day and night (24/7), but certainly at those times when it is reasonable to assume that customers are active.

The strength of webshops lies in the customer recognition and the possibility of communicating directly with them. Webshops obviously have to take advantage of this possibility. In order to do this a good database (CRM system) is essential. The data is collected via the website by asking the customer if they would like to be kept informed of the latest news or special offers. For this the customer would have to tick a box (*opt-in*). And, of course, the customer must always be given the possibility to unsubscribe. Another good method is to ask this question also during the ordering process. If the customer is in a buying mood he will probably choose to be kept informed. The customer details must be used for targeted, customised communication as much as possible, not only about products but also about general (interest) information such as described above. With large address databases it is possible to carry out effective analyses of the customer behaviour as well as make profiles of customers that display the same behaviour. In this way, it is possible to make a good prediction of the future behaviour of customers. Marketing makes use of target groups. These are often objectively determined (predefined) groups formed on the basis of objective characteristics such as gender, age and income. As the behaviour of customers on the Internet is actually still being registered, this can form the basis for determining these target groups. What time does someone visit a website, how long does he stay on the site, what does he look at and what does he buy? These are all behaviour-linked criteria that form the basis of a (post-determined) profile. It helps to better predict the possible buying behaviour and future visiting behaviour. It all becomes very simple once a customer is willing to login; a unique link between a person and the behaviour can then be made. What's more, cookies can be used to automatically recognise and identify a returning visitor. This personal identification, followed by analyses and communication, is the main strength of webshops compared with physical shops. A physical shop would only have this information if they were to register both when a customer entered the shop and what they did while being in the shop (see Chapter 6 New Concepts).

Conversion

Once the visitor is on the website it must be clear what he wants. There are various types of sites:

- communication sites, such as blogs and video sites

- information sites that want to say more about shops such as opening hours, the products available and where they can be bought

- community sites such as social media

- social shopping sites

- the so-called transaction sites

For visitors the objective of a website must be clear. Information sites for example have to provide clear information about products, services or the shops, as well as links to other sites for additional information. A transaction site should focus on realising the transaction. So from the moment a customer visits the website he should be motivated to buy, and tempted to buy even more. Clear product information and product recognition, special offers, the latest additions to collections and suggestions based on the customer's historical behaviour or previous purchases all help in this. The transaction should proceed smoothly and provide clear information regarding delivery and prices. The website should avoid long lists of questions, and the buyer should not have to go through too many steps and windows. A transaction entails purchase, delivery and payment. All other information is often viewed as an irritation. In order to achieve a good conversion the customer must be guided quickly through the transaction, and rational information should be provided as well as assist in the purchase. Product suggestions, special offers such as extra discount if more than one product is bought, extra product information and delivery conditions (free delivery) all help to contribute to a positive purchase decision. It must be made clear and easy for the buyers. They should be provided with assistance in their purchases and care should be taken in giving appropriate suggestions. It really is that simple. Determine whether you need to appeal more to the rational mind, such as with blog sites, or more to the emotion, as is the case with fashion websites. Particularly websites dealing with babies or children products are much more successful if they appeal to the emotions of the buyers. The new suppliers in this market are often young mothers themselves who are passionate about their product. They try to achieve a strong personal bond by using their own name and displaying photos of their own children. In this way, they hope to create a strong emotional bond with the target group, other young mothers. This is an example of intrinsic entrepreneurship, whereby the supplier is motivated and strongly involved with the product. And it is these emotional qualities that can make these entrepreneurs a success.

The opportunities for webshops particularly lie in rational thinking and customer recognition and also increasingly more in the social bonding with the target group as described above. Webshops should capitalise on the limitations of the physical shops and so focus on their advantages compared to physical shops, such as quick response to emails, constant accessibility, speedy deliveries and targeted, personal and relevant communication, customisation, practically unlimited product range and no restrictions in terms of location, delivery times or payment conditions. And finally the home-shopping guarantee hallmark guarantees standard conditions of delivery which gives clarity and creates trust.

PROBLEMS WITH WEBSHOPS

On the face of it starting a webshop may seem an excellent idea, but in most cases this is not necessarily so. The weaknesses of webshops are often also the strong points of the physical shops, and it is here where the battleground lies. It is not that difficult to make a website. There are many good companies that for a reasonable price can create a layout for you, and there is also plenty of standard software available that can provide the necessary IT support for the website (front office processes). Such supporting processes include logistics, payment and operation functions, such as finance, mailing, stock control and purchasing. This software often also contains marketing modules for emails, newsletters, analyses and alerts. The price varies depending on the required functionality. When choosing the software it is very important to have a clear idea of what you really need: functions, modules, scope and intensity. But the business operations only truly begin once the webshop is ready. How do you find your visitors, how do you keep them on your website, how do you turn a visitor into a customer (conversion) and how do you ensure that they return. These are considerable problems for webshop businesses. You can't really miss a local shop; you regularly walk passed it and may hear people talk about it.

On the Internet, however, you don't really just come across a webshop; you have to make a conscious decision to go there. Experienced Internet users have their own preferences, their own addresses for particular products. Through regular communication and frequent visits to a website a casualness arises. This is also the advantage that market leaders enjoy as well as those websites that appeal to a broad public. Well-known mail-order companies appeal to us all and through its background as a mail-order company has built up a good awareness amongst potential customers. At the start eBay and e.g. lastminute. com enjoyed a great deal of publicity, which helped them gain a degree of awareness amongst customers far greater than the other classified ad sites that started later. If you do not enjoy the benefit of publicity, you have to create traffic in another way. For this it is important that there is a clear association between the domain name and your products. You also have to ensure that there is a spontaneous confrontation and you have regular and targeted communication with your target group. There are many possibilities open for realising this. They must, however, be applied effectively, consciously and intensively. Here are just a few:

- Ensure that you are high on the list of search results with Google/ Bing.

- Use your customer database for regular communication. This will attract customers to your website (for example a message or newsletter every two weeks).

- Ensure that the website is regularly kept up to date, on a weekly basis for instance.

- Ensure that you have relevant links on other websites (affiliates).

- Ensure that you have an active social media policy. This can be Facebook, on which you can set up a separate fan page for users who wish to be kept up to date. You can also try to attract many followers and search for new members. You can post various photos and videos, thereby encouraging this group to also share information with one another.

- Ensure you have fun videos on YouTube or other relevant websites, including, of course, your own site.

- Ensure you are mentioned on blogs and other newsletters, and that you are active on popular microblogging sites such as Twitter.

- A Twitter strategy is aimed at creating as many followers as possible. Provide interesting tweets, thereby creating leads to your own site.

- Create news that is picked up by news sites.

- Communicate often and extensively. This does not have to be about your own company, but it can be about other related subjects that the potential visitor may find interesting.

- Analyse where visitors come from and what they look at on the website. This provides a great deal of information about the interests of the visitor, but also about sites that can be given more attention as *lead generator*. Consult, for example, Google analytics regularly.

- Ensure that the website is a pleasant experience for the visitor: not too much text, plenty of pictures and videos. Make sure the visitor does not have to scroll. It is better to click on links for more information. This is more pleasant for the visitor and also gives more information regarding the visitor's viewing and clicking behaviour.

- In some cases an RSS-feed can be handy, as this uses an external information source of which the information is automatically displayed on the company's own site. This naturally makes the website even more up to date.

In short, ensure that the attention of your potential visitors is drawn to your website (company name and link) and that the site is actually worth the visit. Make sure it has the latest news and is regularly kept up to date. Direct, personal communication is the key to success.

The website must meet the visitors' expectations. Information sites should provide good information, have a clear search structure and provide links to relevant sites and suppliers. A good example of this is the medical websites that provide information about physical ailments or injuries. These sites have to provide relevant information regarding the causes, symptoms and treatment. Any links to a specialist or to information regarding medication would be considered a much-appreciated service. Suppliers can take advantage of this opportunity and jump on the bandwagon. The visitors' expectations of the type of website have to be taken into consideration: an orientation site, and information site or a transaction site. Most webshops are transaction sites where particular products can be bought. Product information is often provided as well. This is the traditional approach: buy products and acquire product information. Based on specific needs a person first looks for information. It is therefore understandable that there are specific information websites. These sites claim to provide objective information about particular subjects. As a service to visitors links can be provided to other sites, often webshops. A webshop may deliberately choose to have alongside the webshop a number of information sites that provide general objective information and specific links to the webshop.

The Internet as New Shopping Street?

Internet sales are steadily on the rise and the expectations are unanimously positive. Customers are getting accustomed to shopping whilst sat comfortably on the sofa in front of the television, the speedy deliveries and the 'money back guarantee'. People are deciding to buy on the Internet in increasing numbers. And on top of this, customers are also becoming increasingly disappointed by the existing retail shops when they do not receive the same service there as they do on the Internet, or if the shop does not meet their expectations. For suppliers this is a real dilemma, because how can you provide extra service and yet still continue to make a profit? How can you continue to compete with Internet shops on the basis of price and opening hours; because how can shops stay open longer without incurring extra costs, and, above all, will customers still continue to buy at the shop?

In addition to the above, the occasional empty shop in the shopping street is not particularly inviting for potential shoppers. The products offered in the traditional shopping street are becoming increasingly less varied, and customers come because they have to, not because they enjoy it. And since customers also go to shops less frequently because of the alternative shopping options, such as the Internet or shops much further away, the traditional shopping concept is under pressure even further. What's more, the value of product brands is, of course, an important factor, as the buying behaviour on the Internet often involves buying product brands. This will lead to a decrease in value of the physical sales outlets for brand manufacturers:

- Brands will want to pay less for the space they rent in the department store.

- Brands will consider setting up their own shop which would be able to position their brand even better and where the atmosphere and experience can be demonstrated.

- Brands will actually focus more on the Internet.

The Internet forms such a great threat as customers these days shop online as an alternative to traditional shopping. The buying behaviour online is different, but the Internet does also influence the shopping behaviour as described earlier. This development is leading to less appealing department stores, fewer buying public and less turnover for the shop. Increasing numbers of empty premises can be seen on the high street, which can only result in the shopping street losing its appeal – a vicious circle.

EMPTY PREMISES ALSO A THREAT FOR SHOPS

Shop properties, as is the case with the office market, are threatening to be hit by overproduction and lack of control. The Dutch shop register Locatus expects that in 2020 an average of 1 in 10 shops will be empty.

- *In a number of Dutch provinces the level of empty premises could reach up to 30% if no action is taken. At the start of this year the figure was 6%.*

- *The Dutch Association of Institutional Investors in Property fears that a misplaced optimism of investors for shop properties is leading to an overproduction. In contrast offices and housing are not being built due to forecasts showing unfavourable times.*

- *The rise of the Internet*

- *The Netherlands has the largest number of shop metres per capita of all the countries in Europe, reveal figures from the property agents Jones LaSalle. Due to the ageing population and the rise of the Internet, in the future there'll be less of a need for shops. The Dutch Bank recently warned about the consequences of overvaluing commercial property.*

Temporary measures to give a full shop appearance include jacketing, photo covering, webshop-shopwindows with QR codes and pop-up stores only open for a short time

Source: FD.nl, 23 May 2011.

Shops have to create benefits and provide extra value through the advice, presence of physical products or the experience that they provide. Webshops are creative, however, and are constantly eroding this extra value of the traditional shops. Information can be found on the Internet increasingly easy, there is now far greater trust in webshops and it is convenient buying from home. Shop owners, of course, blame the Internet for the empty shops, but as we have already seen that is not really a fair accusation. There are various influences that have a negative effect on the shopping behaviour and the products offered in the shops, and the Internet is just one of them. Physical restrictions, local council policy, limited opening hours and the often rigid attitude of shopkeepers do not help to encourage people to come to the shop. What's more, the other role of suppliers, who no longer see the retailer as a partner but as the competition, makes collaboration more difficult. And then there is the technology that is increasingly making physical products virtual, as we now see happening with newspapers, news provision and books.

VIRTUAL PRODUCTS

For virtual products it is no longer necessary for customers to go to a shop. They can simply be downloaded. This situation leads to a change in the products that are sold in shops; there are now fewer music shops, bookshops and electronics shops. But will the Internet become the new shopping street? I think that is very unlikely. The Internet, too, has some shortcomings when it comes to shopping, as already described earlier. Shopping on the Internet is not really that much fun; it is mainly convenient. It can be difficult to create emotion in a webshop. And it is difficult to make shopping on the sofa fun; all that Internet visitors do there is surf from shop to shop, which is often not that much fun in a shopping street either. The Internet is handy, rational and convenient, but shopping in physical shops can be a recreational activity. And this is the secret ingredient of the retail trade, and therefore the solution for its future.

Customers weigh up the pros and cons and buy quickly on the Internet if they know what they want.

> Clothing brand Turnover has stopped its webshop operations. This decision was made this week as the brand wishes to focus completely on its wholesale activities and sales in physical shops. Turnover articles can now only be bought online from Orangebag.nl.

Source: FashionUnited, 10 June 2011.

COLLABORATION BETWEEN MANUFACTURER AND DEALER

Brand manufacturers can sell on the Internet, but they don't necessarily have to. If the physical elements are important then the shop has significant value. However, if the retail trade is to be stimulated in particular then making a clear choice is important, like Turnover has done. Bose, too, has decided to sell its audio equipment through authorised dealers, because it was felt that this was the best way to provide information and to demonstrate the superior sound quality of Bose. The Internet provides information on the Bose products and details on the nearest dealer. This is an example of good collaboration. For AutoStyle dealers, a Dutch car accessory company, the Internet is also an additional channel. Customers can search for information on AutoStyle products as well as order online, but at all times the local dealer is the service point from which they can collect the products or get support with assembly. This creates a win-win situation. The strong aspects of the Internet are the information function and the possibility of ordering products directly. Buyers have the choice to either have the products delivered to their home or to collect them from the service point. Certainly if they require a combination of information, ordering, advice and collection, then this is the logical choice. If they know exactly what they need, they can order this directly on the Internet and have it delivered to their home. If there are any problems or difficulties they can always go to their local service point!

AUSTRALIAN RETAIL BATTLES AGAINST FOREIGN E-COMMERCE

> Australian retailers have introduced charges for trying on clothes for size, in order to dissuade customers from then leaving the shop to order the articles online. Consumers in a number of ski shops, for example, have to pay a $50 fee for trying on ski boots. If they buy the

product, however, they get their money back. Other physical retailers are adopting this trend, as over the last few years they have suffered a loss of income as a result of the popularity of e-commerce.

The retailers have demanded that the government remove tax benefits currently enjoyed by the overseas retail trade. This benefit involves foreign online retailers not having to pay 10% VAT on the imported goods nor the 10 to 15% import duties on items less than $1,000. According to Bill Shorten, Minister of Economic Affairs, traditional retailers are still ahead of their online retail competition thanks to their customer service. 'You can compete on more than price alone,' says Shorten in a letter to the International Fashion Group. 'Consumers may find cheaper products online, but they will simply have to forego the personal service or advice.'

The International Fashion Group has responded angrily to the letter of Bill Shorten. 'Consumers are going to shops to try on certain brands, then leave empty handed to later buy online from the US,' says David Mendels in The Weekend Australian. 'An item of clothing that is bought abroad doesn't bring any money into the country.'

Source: *Daily Telegraph* and Retailnews.nl, 15 April 2011.

NEW CUSTOMERS THROUGH COLLABORATION

The charm of a shopping street depends on the diversity of the products being sold. There can be different types of shops alongside a chip shop or a sandwich bar, shops selling expensive items, shops with cheaper products. This diversity is attractive, but the public is important as well. A busy shopping street has a good atmosphere. You don't find this on the Internet. There is a new concept, however, that responds to this demand for fun and pleasant shopping, and this is called *social shopping*. Living Social and Groupon are both examples of this. Here people can talk to one another about a product (chat function and guestbook), but also order together. The more people who order, the cheaper the product. Associated with this concept is a certain *shopping window*, a time frame in which to buy. However social this may be, it is, of course, never quite the same as going shopping together in the town centre. Registering for products with people you don't know is really a form of greed, with the aim of getting a discount. And so the social aspect has again become a rational one.

Other initiatives are based on *co-browsing,* where you can search together for other websites or products. On the Internet this still feels very contrived, but in the real world it is a reality, where the Internet can actually add some value, as will be described in the next chapter. A limited form of social shopping is shown on guestbooks and messages on blogs and microblogs such as Twitter. A guestbook is a spontaneous registry of other buyers, who are keen to share their opinions with others regarding products or (web)shops. In this way, they can influence the buying behaviour of other people. It is quite striking to see all the positive reports in the guestbooks. Can it be that there are only satisfied customers or do the suppliers closely monitor these guestbooks? Social media like Facebook have the same effect. Customers can talk about the shop or products and the owner can see what motivates the customer.

On Twitter this is different. There the users speak without restraint about their experiences, both positive and certainly also negative. In this way, followers are stimulated to share their experiences or to even take a look at the shop or the product suppliers. Twitter is a general platform with followers, whilst for example portals or communities are based on a theme. Suppliers are recommended (portals) and users are attracted on the basis of an area of interest. In portals it is mainly the suppliers who collaborate in order to make what's being offered more transparent. There are, for example, holiday portals, which provide information on holiday destinations, but also provide direct links to relevant sites of travel agents, travel information or travel accessories. This in effect creates a sort of 'theme street' where all suppliers that are related to a particular theme can offer their products. The combination of theme, the advertising of the portal and the higher ranking in search engines attract customers. A clear win-win situation for suppliers and customers alike. It is certainly not an old-fashioned shopping street but a modern themed related supply of products.

> *Four out of 10 shops will have to shut in the next five years as consumers turn their backs on traditional stores in favour of online shopping, according to a report which casts more doubt on the future of the beleaguered British high street.*

> *With retail experts increasingly painting a picture of a future high street lined with coffee shops and internet kiosks, a report from Deloitte highlights how the boundaries between physical and virtual space are becoming blurred with thousands of shops likely to face closure in coming years.*

To remain competitive, retailers may have to reduce their property portfolios by 30–40% in the next five years and adapt what remains to meet the changing demands of consumers, Deloitte said. The growing trend in the US for large warehouse-style retail outlets to have free instore Wi-Fi to help customers shop online is expected to spread around the world. Tesco has already announced plans for such facilities in its UK stores.

'The majority of UK retailers have simply got too many stores,' said Silvia Rindone, a director in the retail consulting practice at Deloitte and author of the Store of the Future report. Total floor space has dropped in recent years, she noted, and this will continue as consumers shop more on the internet, with online sales forecast to reach £43bn by 2015, accounting for 14% of all retail sales. Some 22% of people did not buy their last item of clothing or accessories in store, and only 9% of customers want to see the full product range in shops.

Source: Julia Kollewe, Deloitte Report, guardian.co.uk, 20 March 2012.

COMMUNITIES AND LIKE-MINDED PEOPLE

Communities are ideal places for users to find others based on a particular subject or theme. There are communities on Facebook and LinkedIn that have a particular subject as a bonding factor. This may be a brand, a shop but also a particular area of interest. If users have a certain bond with the subject or object, there will be a greater bond between all those involved. These communities usually provide a great deal of information on the subject whilst the users also share their own knowledge. These communities (social media) are characterised by their *user generated content*. Users produce their own content which in turn can be viewed by other users. The Apple brand has gone even further than making the brand experience central. There are various communities that unite users: Apple fanatics, Apple users, software developers or engineers. If there is a problem with your Apple computer or software you can post your question on the community and sometimes within minutes you will get a response from others within that community. In this way the users can solve one another's problems. Apple then only has to monitor this and see whether this is of value to the Apple brand (new releases or information about the experiences of users). The websites of shopping centres can also have a portal function. These sites, however, will have to provide information about the shops, the products sold and opening hours, in order to attract customers to the shopping centre. They should not try to compete with the physical shopping centre, because the reasons for buying on the Internet and the buying experience are, after all, different from those for physical shopping centres. Those websites should therefore attract customers to the shopping centre and just be complementary.

The main differences between online shopping and shopping at physical shops are the reason that people go shopping (rational) and what the customers experience (emotion). Due to these differences, both forms of shopping can easily coexist as well as mutually influence one another. It is therefore wrong to regard the Internet as a competitor of the existing retail or vice versa; they complement one another. As the retail sector had always been there, there was a need to go to the shop. However, due to the Internet it is no longer taken for granted that people shop at physical shops. And this is why the retail sector has to rethink why customers shop. If retailers know the answer, they will be able to respond accordingly. If they do not succeed in this, these particular shops will no longer have a future. On the other hand, the same also applies to webshops. If they do not know why customers visit a website and why customers buy, they will not be able to respond to the specific customer behaviour. Webshops have the advantage, however, that they know why customers visit the website, how long they have stayed there and where they came from. This knowledge can then be used to increase the *sticky factor*, in order to commit visitors.

MOTHERCARE TO CLOSE 110 SHOPS

Mothercare, the largest retailer of baby and children's clothes and accessories in Britain, will close 110 of its shops on Britain's high streets to focus on out-of-town superstores, after a dramatic fall of 73% in profits last year. The company suffered from the bad weather in September 2010 and lower levels of consumer spending. The resulting large stocks were put in the sales of the first quarter of 2011, but did not compensate sufficiently for the loss. This has led to the closure of 110 shops and new negotiations regarding the rental prices of other shops. The business will still retain 266 shops in the UK, 102 of which are in out-of-town shopping centres.

Source: *The Telegraph* online at www.telegraph.co.uk, 18 May 2011.

A New Retail Landscape

A new component has been added to the retail landscape, the Internet. The Internet is an advertising column (the information function) as well as a social medium (the communication function). In addition, products can be bought on the Internet. These three functions can be a threat, but they can also help to complement the existing retail. What is certain is that it has to lead to a change in the retail sector. The circumstances have changed quite radically from how they used to be. Customers have also changed, so it is logical that the retail sector has to change with it. The future lies in *web based retailing*, with the Internet integrated within the retail concept.

The contours of the new retail landscape are now becoming clear: shopping streets with a residential function but where people can also do fun things – go out for a coffee, for meals, and browse in pleasant boutiques and other charming shops. The larger shopping centres out of town are for all other purchases. They provide parking facilities, entertainment and act as a magnet with facilities such as theatres, football stadiums or other attractions. Groceries are bought at the local supermarket, which have plenty of parking space and long opening hours. Shopping is a form of recreation and often an incidental activity that may be done before or after, for example, going to the cinema or restaurant. The IKEA concept, in which the location is less important than the shop experience, will be seen increasingly often. The strong function of the Internet is its information function for the owners of both webshops and physical shops. Customers buy on the Internet on the basis of rational considerations or the service that is provided. They buy in the physical shop because they trust it and the advantage that they can take the products home straightaway. Customers look for information and decide upon which product to buy at home on their iPad or laptop. They then decide whether to go to a physical shop or to place an order on the Internet straightaway. A physical shop enjoys greater awareness amongst potential customers. That is certainly an advantage; however, it has to find out more about this new buying behaviour if it is to be successful on the Internet.

There will, therefore, be three types of players:

- the pure (solely) Internet players in a market dominated by a few powerful parties

- the pure players in the physical world, mainly led by local shops with a local look and feel

- the cross-retail businesses (omni retailing) that are present both physically and on the Internet, sometimes only with information, but sometimes also with a complete Internet strategy.

In view of all this it makes sense that Mothercare is moving to the large shopping centres; there are parking facilities, and customers can turn a visit into a day out with the children. What's more, the appeal of the entire centre is used to attract customers. Department stores will therefore prefer these types of centres, as they will reach a larger public and the problems of city centres (accessibility and parking) don't apply there. This situation, however, will lead to empty properties in the cities and the high streets, which in turn will make these areas less appealing for shopping. The shopping streets as a result will acquire a different function, but is that really so bad if customers want it? City centres can be fun again if they combine small shops, specialised shops that surprise with entertainment, culture and restaurants. Counter-shops have disappeared from the shops, the supermarket has vanished from the city centre, the drapery shop has gone, as well as the music shop and bookshop, but has this made the centre any less attractive to potential customer? By modifying the centres according to the wishes of customers, the demographic developments (more single and older people) and the new way people spend their leisure time (an evolving process) these centres can be made attractive once more. Retailers have to rethink why customers buy and whether the Internet complements or threatens this concept. They must realise that the growing number of older people and single people will prefer city centres because of the entertainment, culture and pubs and restaurants. Going out is more fun in a city centre than in an out of town place for the people. The increasing mobility costs will add to this (cost of petrol). May be this is the future for city centres. Surprise people and make a visit enjoyable.

THE DRAPERY SHOP

How long ago is it that there was a drapery shop in every shopping street? A search on the Internet showed me that there still were many draperies around, but when I looked in the town centre it turned out that they had all closed down the previous year. No more draperies in the city centre, and even in the larger cities it seems that this type of shop has now disappeared from the high street. I finally managed to find a shop in a nearby town. A pleasant old lady served me, but the rolls of fabric were no longer eight metres. 'Can you order more fabric?' 'I can ring the wholesaler on Monday, as long as it does not go bankrupt in the meantime.' 'But surely you can order more fabric?' 'Not really, sir, otherwise everyone in the village would end up walking around in the same dress!'

The new retail landscape is becoming apparent. The new buying behaviour is leading to a different type of product range and shop. The new shopping, which has resulted from this, is leading to a change on the high street. After posting a message on Twitter I was recommended various websites for fabrics within just five minutes. There was a large selection and I had it delivered to my house the following day. The Internet was not a choice when it came to ordering the fabric; it turned out to be a necessity. Perhaps this is an omen for the future of retailing.

Conclusion and Summary of Chapter 4

The Internet provides opportunities, but webshops also have problems that physical shops do not face. Webshops know their customers, but they first have to attract them and win their trust. Physical shops have to learn from this and re-determine the extra value and benefits they can provide.

Table 4.2   Conclusion and summary

Change	Internet	Consequences for retail
Buying behaviour.	Orientation and providing information.	Critical customers, determine once again the advantages.
Buying moment/reasons.	Rational considerations, convenience, unrestricted buying in terms of time and place, possibility to return products, services.	Customers make a conscious choice regarding shop, shopping is becoming a recreational activity, major change in shopping streets, more out-of-town shopping centres.
Experience.	Rational considerations, information, practical.	Pleasant, fun and reliable.
Future.	A few major players, many niche players, existing shops, mainly information websites. Impact social media.	More personal approach and personal communication. Search for magnet/attractions.

5

Technology and Retail: In Times of Change You Have to Get to Know Your Customers

Retailing has traditionally been a concept involving sound buying policy, good business premises and finding the right (sales) location. With its origins in the mobile retailing trade of the Middle Ages,[1] this developed into the shops of the nineteenth century and finally converged into department stores and shopping streets at the start of the twentieth century. The latter phase, now only 40 years old, involved a concentration of shops into shopping centres with pedestrianised areas. Retail is constantly evolving into new concepts in order to attract customers and to supply products that the customers want. After all, if the customer has no interest, the shop will not sell anything. It's as simple as that.

Development of Technology in Retail

Technology was not originally part of retailing. It was only when the electronic till was introduced that the retailer came into contact with technology. As with most innovations, the first phase in the application of technology is aimed at efficiency. This was no different with retail. The electronic till enabled sales transactions to be carried out more quickly and efficiently. Later the bookkeeping became automated, which was then followed by sales automation with the introduction of the bar code. At the same time (at the end of the 1980s), the purchasing process also changed due to the application of EDI (Electronic Data Interchange) and a unique article coding (the unique article number EAN). Thanks to EDI, other kinds of relationships developed between retailers

---

1   For a more detailed description of the history of retailing, read Gartmayr Eduard, *Nicht für den gewinn allein*, 1964, Frankfurt aM: Verlag für Wirtschaftspraxis GmbH.

and suppliers, and a more efficient stock control was made possible. A good coordination between systems, shop and supplier was necessary for this. The EAN was used particularly for cash till transactions and stock administration. This code is a further development of the UPC code and forms the basis of the bar code. Its application led to an improved efficiency and supported the link between systems: the stock, order and purchasing systems. By using the EAN code everyone could refer to the same article. The old structures, however, remained intact: manufacturers for the product, logistics and wholesalers for distribution, and the retailer for selling to the customers. The process simply became more efficient, and the relationship between the various parties in this supply chain closer. In general, the retail sector did not have a great deal of interest in the technology unless it would lead to cost savings. Selling required a good product range, good pricing and good sales staff, which very much suited the old business model.

The use of technology in retail has shifted in recent years from the back office, such as bookkeeping, stock control and purchasing, to the shop, to the actual moment of the sales transaction. The basic retail criteria are changing due to this application of technology, and in particular the technology that customers have adopted. No longer is it merely a question of greater efficiency. It is to do with a different customer relationship. The customer is now no longer the end point of the process, but the start. And it is no longer a question of selling to customers, but enabling customers to buy. Mobile phones, the Internet, smartphones, tablets, Location Based Services and Near Field Communication together with RFID, GPS and online communities are new developments that are important for customers and shopping in the future. The customer's world has changed, as has the customer's behaviour. The retailer can therefore no longer do without technology if he is to attract customers and assist them in buying. But will technology also have to form an important part of modern retailing and the new business model (see the next chapter)?

Attracting Customers

Retailers have to lure customers into the shop with appealing promotions, discounts or deals. An example of this is the discounts that are offered on the Internet (via email). The most well-known parties involved in this are Groupon and Living Social, which are both active and successful internationally. Based on the recipient's location, interesting special deals are received every day. The special deals are only available for a limited time, so speedy action is required.

The payment is made to Groupon or Living Social, after which the customer can go to the shop to pick up the article or use the service. The customers are therefore attracted to the shop, restaurant or theme park by these interesting special deals. The challenge for the retailer then is to sell more and thereby compensate for the costs of this special deal. What's more, the customers now know the shop, so registering an email address or a follow-up promotion can help to encourage customers to return.

These special deal services are costly, particularly for physical products. Not only does a substantial discount have to be given on the products, but also a considerable commission to the organising company. What's more, there is a delay in the eventual payment and the customer's contact details remain the property of the organising company. In this way, Groupon and other such companies have developed an interesting business model and a useful database of customers with information on residential addresses and transactions regarding the special deals. It would, however, be wise for retailers to maintain their own database with customer details and email addresses. In its simplest form, regular emails can be sent to customers. If the customer's buying details are recorded, then it will be possible to send customised emails. This communication would help to create a top-of-mind position and attract customers to the shop.

Moreover, the additional methods of attracting customers are expensive and usually difficult or impossible to measure. Advertisements, media campaigns and door-to-door distribution remain anonymous. The special deals promotions of Groupon and Living Social should be regarded as a form of advertising, whereby costs are only incurred if use is actually made of the special offer. The application is actually quite traditional, namely a special offer via an email. In the near future, however, this will evolve further. In addition to special offers being made based on profile and location (place of residence), one can also choose to follow a particular company or product group and receive special offers from them. A further development towards the smartphone and *location based services* is then just a small step away. As soon as a registered customer is near a particular shop, a message can be sent to the smartphone with a special offer or another specific product. Because the customer is already in the vicinity, extra data traffic can be created for the shop. If the sales staff also know about the special offer for the customer (through automatic recognition), the gap between physical and virtual can be bridged at individual level.

Hyperlocal marketing services are on the verge of a breakthrough. Small and medium-size businesses will have to implement these services themselves as the manual processing would be too expensive to outsource to marketing specialists. Services such as Foursquare, Facebook Places, Google Boost and Google Place Pages offer possibilities to local retailers.

Recent figures have shown that one third to a half of mobile search commands are related to a person's location. Many parties are therefore trying to capitalise on this opportunity. Google has recently introduced a new advertising service Boost onto the market, which is specially designed for small local businesses that are generally not so adept in the new technologies and online advertising.

Source: Emerce.nl, 17 October 2010.

The new shopping involves a combination of the Internet and physical shops. By integrating the Internet within the physical behaviour of customers, a stronger proposition for the existing retail can be created. And in turn, integrating physical elements within the webshops (such as collection points and showrooms) will also strengthen Internet shopping. It is therefore essential that shops, if they are to survive, also integrate the Internet within the shop and, in so doing, respond to the behaviour and the expectations of customers. This does not necessarily involve setting up a webshop; providing information on the shop and perhaps also information on products, possibly in collaboration with other suppliers such as manufacturers, may be sufficient.

Another way of attracting customers is to use the appeal of other sites, for example by collaborating with new concepts or with portals such as those of the local council or a particular business sector, or by using the customers' search behaviour. Getting on top of Google search results is sometimes seen as a solution, but Google is an information source, not a buying channel. Classified ad websites such as Gumtree do, however, attract buyers. The visitors are clearly looking for particular articles, new or second-hand. Shopkeepers can take advantage of this by advertising, or by buying a set place based on certain selection criteria. This set place can then lead to one's own website in order to attract customers to the shop or to sell products directly. Major suppliers also use these sites to make *embedded* special offers. If visitors then click on the special offer, they will immediately be directed to the appropriate article in the webshop of the retailer. For physical retailers this is a good medium for attracting customers; using advanced technology it is possible to attract local visitors and bring their attention to the products on offer at the shop.

Technology in the Shop

The anonymous customer is now identified, the verbal communication is supported by other forms of communication and the *captive customer*, the customer in the shop without external contacts, is becoming a *connected customer*, who is kept in contact with the outside world. This change is essential for physical retailers; the way in which retailers respond to this will determine what sort of future awaits them.

QR CODE

A first step in connecting customers to external sources of information is the Quick Response code. The QR code is a hidden link to a website. The website can contain information on the product or a product comparison, a link to a comparison site or, for example, a video explaining the use of the product. Through a special app (application) on the smartphone or tablet, such as the iPad, a customer takes a photo of the QR code after which a connection is made with the relevant website. This helps the customers make a better choice.

EXAMPLE OF QR CODE

The QR code bridges the gap between the physical products and the physical presence in the shop on the one hand and the possibilities of the Internet on the other. This book also contains various QR codes, making the book no longer static, but interactive. This allows for a multimedia reading experience. By activating the QR code with a smartphone or tablet such as the iPad, customers can view videos regarding the relevant subject straightaway. The links to the relevant websites are static. The site, however, can be dynamic. Videos can be constantly updated without the QR code having to be changed. As a result, the book has changed from a static product to a dynamic one, and can therefore respond to the contemporary situation. I believe that this application is unique in the book world and is an indication for the retail sector how experience and topicality can be added to static shopping.

IPAD

Another possibility is to install a tablet, such as the iPad, in the shop. This would allow the customer to use apps to look for information on the Internet themselves. The iPads are pre-programmed with specific apps that can link to information sites or sections of the retailer's website. This will allow customers to find information more effectively and to order (online) if they so wish. It is, of course, also possible to buy in the shop straightaway. This provides a better customer experience, a feeling of transparency and, naturally, a more effective use of sales staff. Apple provided this service in all its shops during the weekend of 22 May 2011 and linked its entire product range to apps, installing iPads in the shop alongside the relevant products. It is also possible for a salesperson to use an iPad while talking to customers. This would help to reduce errors regarding what's on offer on the Internet (low prices) or misinterpretations regarding information on the products. The integration of the Internet would support the sales pitch, especially if suppliers create a separate web page for supporting shop sales staff. This would bring back harmony between suppliers and shops, in the interest of both parties as well as the customer.

> *Last Sunday Apple fitted out all its Apple stores worldwide with iPad stations next to all its products. These iPad stations function as sales tools and provide support to customers. A new instore app helps to answer customers' questions, which in turn encourages the customers to remain in the shop, instead of them leaving to look further on the Internet at home. If you tap on the customer service icon, a salesperson will come to assist you straightaway. Apple believes that this application should be an example for the rest of the retail sector. Customers have to find their way through the many articles and the commercial deluge of posters and special offers. Searching out a member of sales staff often also leads to irritation amongst customers. Apple regards the iPad application as a way of adding personal experience to the traditional way of shopping. It wishes to approach the shops in the same way as its devices. By using technology and software, customers can be offered the ultimate experience.*

> *Apple is also expanding the product presentations and workshops in the retail stores. The company will continue with the workshops for film editing and digital photo editing, but will expand them with workshops for the iPhone and iPad, the 'Tips and tricks workshops'. In this way, Apple wants to be an example to the retail sector by showing that the shop has to change along with the changes in the customers' wishes and behaviour. By applying technology from the perspective of the user, a fun buzz can be created in the shop again.*

> *Source: USA Today, 24 May 2011, Money, section A.*

INFORMATION TERMINALS

A variant of the applications of the iPad or other tablets are the information terminals in shops. At these terminals a customer can independently, or with the assistance of a salesperson, look for products and information, and even place orders. These terminals are linked to the shop's product range and website. If products are not available in the shop they can be ordered directly. It is also possible to expand the product range offered in the shop, which is always limited due to lack of space, with an unlimited range of products on the Internet. In addition to the shop's normal product range, this can also include products from associated partners. These information terminals were at first vertical screen, however customer did not find this very pleasant because they fear other customers can look as well on the screen. This vertical screen has now often been replaced by an inclined screen, which provides not only greater ease of use for the customer but also, in particular, more privacy. Customers can look for information on products at their leisure, view the products and evaluate them. If they wish, they can order them (or buy them and take them home straightaway). In this way a retailer can expanded the shop's product range with many more products than would be physically achievable in the shop itself. The sales staff can assist the customer in selecting the product by providing advice. This helps to gain the customer's trust. They can, of course, also look on the Internet together with the customer. This helps to bridge the gap between the physical shop and the products available online. It would, therefore, no longer be necessary for customers to look further on the Internet when they are back home; that can already be done in the shop. This service will help to reduce the number of customers who go into the shop for advice but then leave without buying anything.

DIGITAL PRICE TAGS

An example of the application of technology in the shop is the digital tags you get with products containing product information and retail price. This digital tag differs from the traditional information label or plate in that this digital application can be fed with information centrally, as well as from another source. Links can be made with, for example, comparison sites which would allow specific comparison data to be presented. The customers would become better informed, and perhaps buy more quickly. This technology can also be used in fashion shops. Clothes are not bought just like that; usually the customer would want the advice of a friend. By sending a friend a photo of the mirror image of the customer wearing the item of clothing, he or she would be able to give advice immediately. By fitting the mirror with a photo function, it can send the photo by email to a particular email address, Twitter account or Facebook page.

> *Fashion shop WE has installed a Twitter mirror in a number of its branches throughout Europe,' announces electronics company Nedap.*

> *Using the Tweet mirror you can take a picture in the fitting room of you wearing the item of clothing you intend to buy. Through a touchscreen and Internet connection you can send the photos to your Twitter or Facebook account. Your friends and other followers would then be able to give their opinion directly. For this mirror Nedap received the 'Digital Award 2010' in the 'Best interactive' category for the most revolutionary and innovative product.*

Technology in the Supermarket

The developments in the supermarket differ from those outlined above. This is mainly due to the fact that purchases in a supermarket are routine ones and require little advice. In supermarkets customers prefer efficiency in their purchase transactions. For one thing, the technology there is aimed at efficient order services (no large stocks and no sold-out products) and speedy transactions at the checkout. The ordering procedures have already been optimised throughout the years using the EAN code and EDI. Hand scanners have since helped to bring about further efficiency improvements. The shopkeeper only had to scan the bar code and enter the number of items. The package sizes were already pre-programmed and the order could be sent automatically. By scanning the incoming orders, the correctness of the deliveries could be verified immediately. In the last few years other concepts have been introduced, such as Vendor Managed Inventories (VMI). Here the stocks are the responsibility of the supplier and remain the property of the supplier until the moment they are sold. It is also possible that they remain the property of the retailer, but that the supplier is responsible for the speedy replenishment and deliveries. The supplier is able to determine the stocks for each shop as he also receives information on the numbers sold. The stocks minus the sales determines the invoice amount, as well as the further supplies of the products. Thanks to the use of this technology, ever-increasing efficiency has improved stock control and ordering procedures. What's more, the relationship between supplier and retailer has become closer.

> *Street One is an example of a brand that for years has been able to use the VMI model to achieve demonstrably high returns with its basics on*

external shop floors. The participating mono-brand and multi-brand retailers are able to achieve extremely high turnovers per square metre with this, and there is hardly any more need for markdowns.

Source: Fashionunited indicia B.V.

SMART SHELVING AND RFID

Another application of technology can be found in shops. This takes the form of *smart shelving*, which experiments with the automatic registration of shop stocks. If the minimum level is reached, a purchasing or a replenishment notification is sent immediately. *Smart shelving* is based on RFID technology.[2]

For customers, the queues at the checkouts can sometimes be a real source of irritation. It is possible to eventually solve this through the automatic registration of purchases. All products can be fitted with a chip (RFID) which is registered the moment the products are placed in the shopping trolley. A quick verification can be carried out at the checkout by scanning the entire trolley (takes one second) and then the customer can pay straightaway (see new forms of payment in Chapter 6). This technology is already available. However, as products are still given bar codes, the solution for the time being has been found in self-scanning. Tesco in the UK has introduced this self-scanner which allows customers to scan the items themselves and then pay for them directly. Each item is scanned separately and then placed in the bagging area. Once finished, the customer pays for the total amount. At the Albert Heijn in the Netherlands the bonus card is first scanned and then a scanner allocated. Each item is scanned separately and then placed in the shopping trolley. When the shopping is done, the scanner is read and the customer is asked to select the preferred method of payment. Once paid, the gate opens and the customer can leave the shop without having even spoken to the cashier. These two examples help to reduce the queues for those who do prefer to pay in the traditional manner, or like the contact with the cashier. It also takes advantage of the buying behaviour even before the customer enters the shop. On the Albert Heijn website the customer can do the shopping by indicating the items that he or she wants to buy. On the website suggestions are given on the basis of past buying behaviour. A shopping list can then be printed out based on the most efficient shopping route in the local Albert Heijn shop. Not only can the shopping list be printed out, but the smartphone (or tablet) can also function as a shopping list. The combination of smartphone and shopping list is therefore

---

2   R. Want, 2004, A Key to Automatic Everything. *Scientific American*, 290 (1): 56.

the mobile application for preparing to do the shopping (on the computer or smartphone/tablet, shopping with a list or the smartphone/tablet). It is only a small step to actually paying using your smartphone.

DETERMINING SHOPPING ROUTE

The supermarket is a shop for routine purchases. There is a difference between your weekly routine shopping, which has to be carried out as efficiently as possible, and shopping when this involves looking, choosing, assessing and then finally buying. As a result, the technology used in the supermarket will be different from that in other shops. The role of the Internet will also be different. On the Internet, supermarkets focus on the information function and so show, for example, opening hours, special offers and other specific information. For supermarkets, online shopping is a rather limited application, and is one usually borne out of necessity: people with disabilities, the elderly as well as people with very little time. The majority, however, continue going to the supermarket out of convenience, the freshness of the products and the social aspect. There you see other people, talk to acquaintances and get a feeling of belonging. These human feelings remain important. In addition to the abovementioned groups that do wish to buy on the Internet and have their groceries delivered to their home, there is also an online market for special products, such as special wines, special diet food and food supplements. These products are usually not available locally, so the Internet provides a solution for this.

The applications of technology in supermarkets are based on the core process: purchasing, stocks and sales. The current innovation in this area is the customer's involvement with self-scanning.

The application of identification, as employed by the Albert Heijn website AH.nl, is the first step towards the new possibilities aimed at the individual customer. Customer recognition is necessary for this. This is possible through the smartphone, which can support the buying process, a technology employed by Albert Heijn. An automatic recognition of customers (and products) is possible using an RFID chip.

RFID

For years now Radio Frequency Identification has been regarded as a promising future innovation for shopping. The RFID chip makes it possible to register and identify products and people in a contact-free manner. The RFID chip sends out a signal which when received allows the location to be determined and authorisation given. There are two types of RFID chips: an active chip and a passive chip. The active chip has its own power supply, allowing it to constantly transmit a signal that can be received (possibly through the mobile network) by a receiver. In the case of a passive chip the power supply necessary to transmit the signal is provided by the receiver. The receiver sends out a signal to which the chip responds. The chip normally has a code that can be verified against the details in the database. This allows the code to be identified and then authorisation determined. It is also possible to link the code to location details. The chip is very small, the size of a grain of sand, which allows it to be placed in groceries and clothing. These RFID chips are already used in numerous access control systems. The RFID chip can also be attached to products in order to prevent theft. If a product were to be taken through the gates of a shop without having been paid for, an alarm will be set off. Other information can also be stored on the chip. For example, information on the date, location and time of production, the temperature of the transport (in the case of foodstuffs), the ingredients (taking allergies into account) and the shelf life. In the shop the chip can store information on the date of arrival, the sell-by date and the movements of the product. This would provide details on how often a product is taken off the rack or shelf, how often it is tried on (clothes) or the materials from which it is made. An exciting application is the combination of the chip in an item of clothing and a mirror functioning as a receiver. For each item of clothing the possible accessories or advice on other articles can be displayed on the mirror. This would therefore be similar to webshops where other items are suggested that can also be bought. The suggestions can be matching items or items that other customers had bought at the same time as the product in question. This creates a model identical to that on the Internet, with a system of advice to which the customer is already accustomed. Although these chips are already widely used, their breakthrough in the retail sector is being delayed through their relatively high costs in comparison with bar codes. A bar code costs practically nothing, whereas a chip costs a few cents or pennies. The infrastructure is also hampering its implementation. Bar codes are often already printed on a label or sticker at the factory, whilst a retailer would have to attach the chip himself. Once manufacturers and importers start to attach the chips themselves as well as facilitate the necessary infrastructure (readers and databases), adoption by the retail sector will increase rapidly.

Digital Signage

Many shops employ a form of *digital signage* whereby visitors can see a video about their products. This application only plays if customers are nearby.

Digital signage mainly focuses on products and product presentations, the traditional approach of the retail sector. By using the latest technology, it will be possible to show presentations that are more customised and targeted. The card allows for identification, but this can, of course, also be done through NFC or RFID. Customers would then be able to receive direct personal messages or personal special offers once they are in the shop. These messages are generated based on knowledge about the customer. And this does not, of course, have to be communicated through a public screen. More privacy is possible through a terminal or through the customer's own smartphone. Digital signage 2.0 will no longer be product-oriented but will be targeted at the individual.

Personal Identification

In addition to having the chip attached to articles, it can also be used as a means of personal identification. By integrating the chip in the mobile phone, the power supply of the telephone can be used and the identification can take place more easily. These days almost everybody carries a mobile phone with them all the time. The combination of smartphone and RFID chip is certainly an interesting one. Specific RFID chips can transmit signals with a limited reach, thereby making Near Field Communication possible. This involves communication between mobile phones and transmitters over a small area, but specifically based on personal wishes or profiles. Based on a person's presence in a particular area, services can be offered such as information or videos. For business club members at a sports event, a personal service can be developed based on the wishes of the member. This may be a connection with other members of the club whereby a signal is given if other members are present; a connection with a social medium is a simple application. This ensures that only those members of your network that are nearby are notified. You would then be able to communicate with them directly. Linking location to personal database details, such as a social medium, leads to physical transparency. The smartphone can also function as an admission ticket.

Visitors to a shopping centre would be able to receive information on the shops as well as special offers. All that one would have to do is click on a special app. As soon as they are within the specific area, they would receive the relevant information. This application is interesting to the retail sector, as NFC would be able to be used both in an individual shop and the entire shopping centre. By registering the identification details (such as the number of the chip) in the customer database, historical data can also be used, such as recent purchases. This can form the basis of a loyalty programme. The current generation of loyalty programmes still rely too much on identification at the checkout, the end of the purchasing process. The only possibility then is to offer a discount. If the identification were to take place earlier in the purchasing process, which, as we have seen, can be done with NFC, then a customer upon entering the shop could be identified as a participant in the loyalty system (and his level in the system determined). Other forms of loyalty, such as services, a free cup of coffee, free parking and extra support from sales staff can then be offered. The next chapter will take a closer look at this.

The application of RFID can also lead to specific, location-based services. At the basis of NFC is a combination of communication in a particular area aimed at identified visitors. Location is central to NFC, whereby generic services are offered, such as repeated clips of football matches or general special offers aimed at visitors to a shopping centre. Retailers have to be creative and take a closer look at the possibilities and wishes of the customers. Simply offering Wi-Fi to allow customers to get onto the Internet with a smartphone or tablet is not enough. After all, they can already do that with their own mobile phone subscription. It is with NFC and LBS that you can truly add some value to the shop visit and buying moment.

Apps, Mobile Applications

Smartphones and tablets are computers that have a specific purpose, whereby programs can be activated by touching the screen. With other computers a command has to be typed in, making the keyboard essential. However, with these devices the command is hidden in a pictogram which can be activated by touch. Once this is done a program is started up on the smartphone or an address is looked up on the Internet. This is the same principle as with a QR code. On a webpage there is then specific information, which can also be approached in an interactive manner. This could be navigation information, but also information on restaurants and shops. In this way, it is possible, for example, to book a table, reserve tickets or buy something. The app provides access to information and makes interaction possible. In addition to these touch commands, it also offers a limited typing function. For shops it is important to have an app as well or to be linked to a relevant site (app-controlled). If a shop has its own app, then specific information can be given about the shop or a shopping route can be advised. In order to appeal to customers, it is advisable to constantly keep up-to-date with, for example, deals of the day, menu of the day, or to promote the new collection or range. The disadvantage of an app is, of course, that you have to tap it. However, the combination of a locator and app enables the customer to consult specific messages once near the shop. It is also possible to have a link with a navigation system. Furthermore, there are apps that are based on a location or city. This allows customers to search according to a particular product, shop or attraction. So if they are looking for a shop that sells a particular brand, they will be shown all the shops in the particular area. This, of course, requires discipline from the retailer to ensure that the correct information is given. Other possible applications are the nearest hotel, restaurant or car park.

These days there are also apps that are bound to a particular city or area. Many cities have their own specific apps. These provide information on restaurants, shops, events as well as promotions. For retailers it is important to put these new sources of location-based services to good use, in order to attract and inform customers. This provides an integration of online information with a physical presence. It is often advisable to make use of a certain physical centre of attraction such as a city, event, restaurants and bars. Customers are attracted to these and will regard shopping as part of their leisure time. People may go to a particular city because it is pleasant, organises various events, has cosy bars and restaurants and various local attractions such as a zoo, museums, etc. Shops are part of a day out, not the reason for going out in the first place. By taking advantage of the magnet function of these attractions and coming up with specific offers or information, the attraction can be used to bring in visitors. 'We could pop into town, have a bite to eat at IKEA or just have a look around.' The app of the attraction leads the way. Shopping has become a form of recreation and secondary activity, but shops have to realise this and respond appropriately.

Social Media

The role of social media can sometimes be exaggerated. According to research carried out by Forrester, only 10% of visitors to a social media site occasionally click on a commercial offer or go to a commercial site. With Google this is 70%. That is not to say, however, that social media are not important for the retail sector. Social media have a number of advantages:

- they allow products to be seen and provide a visual meeting with the website or the owner;

- they strengthen the relationship with business contacts and consequently enable direct communication with them;

- social media can be linked to NFC and LBS as well as in-store facilities;

- social media can be useful for tests and consultations;

- direct feedback through *user generated content*.

In this case we specifically deal with the application of social media for the retail sector. Although this specifically refers to the physical, traditional retail sector, most of the applications apply to webshops as well.

Twitter is a phenomenon that allows direct contact between the sender and the receiver. Using short messages (with a maximum of 140 characters) messages can be sent to followers. The followers can in turn respond to the sender. In this way, direct and targeted communication is created. As these are short messages, we refer to microblogs, in contrast to the lengthier messages on blogs to which readers can also respond. Blogs can be integrated into a website, allowing detailed information to be given on products, fashion developments for the new collection, etc. In the case of microblogging such as on Twitter, sending is an important component: saying what is on your mind. Each participant has followers who have chosen to follow a person's messages or a particular company. Everyone who sees a message (tweet) can respond to it, and so a conversation starts between the sender and the reader. This may be customers talking to one another, but also customers in conversation with the supplier. Businesses carry out an automated search for their name, which results in an immediate notification if someone mentions their name. This can be done with a hashtag (#), whereby all tweets that have such a hashtag are grouped together, but also by searching for particular words. Searching on the basis of words is done through a search command. The retailer of a brand is therefore able to have direct insight into what customers say about them and so give an immediate response. It is also possible to forward a message to all your followers. If you receive an interesting or funny message from a user you are following, you can forward this to your own followers, who can in turn forward it themselves. In just a short time, vast numbers of people would have read the message. In this way, news can spread extremely quickly, both positive news and negative news. Twitter played an important role in the recent upheavals and revolutions in the Middle East. Sometimes serious accidents can be reported more quickly on Twitter than on any other news source. Suppliers and manufacturers can use this application to inform large numbers of people very quickly. They would, however, have to be careful with commercial promotions, as these can have a negative impact. At the moment, it is a hype to get as many followers as possible (quantity instead of quality) and award prizes for the umpteenth follower as an incentive to follow. Sometimes people re-tweet too much, which can result in a sort of spam on Twitter. But ultimately the choice of who is followed and what is done on Twitter lies with the user. For businesses this is a good way of maintaining contact with followers/customers and seeing what these customers/Twitterers think about. For larger organisations it is important to take a more professional approach. Customers, after all, do like to complain on Twitter, so a speedy response is necessary. A marketing department therefore has to have social media specialists.

COMMUNITIES

In addition to this direct communication (blogs and microblogs), there are also social media that can connect and bond people. As described in Chapter 1, there are various elements (magnet functions) that can help bring people together, for example a sport, a school, a brand or a company. Through social media sites such as Myspace and Facebook, groups of bonded and like-minded people can be created who are able to meet one another on such sites. Here they can communicate with one another by chatting and posting messages, as well as share photos. Brands and companies can acquire their own group of loyal customers in the same way. This not only helps to reinforce the brand image but also allows the behaviour of customers to be followed. A good example is the many football fan pages found within the social media sites. Top global brands such as Mercedes can boast 3,300,000 and Gucci well over 5,000,000. This creates a large community of like-minded people who have an interest or affinity with the shop or brand. They inform one another, talk about the shop or the brand and share photos and videos. What's more, for smaller shops this is a good opportunity to keep in contact with individual customers. Through Twitter, for example, they can post the occasional message (or even each day) or inform customers about special offers. Shops can, of course, also make use of the appeal of other sites by advertising or being active on them, for example brand sites or the sites of the local council of the city in which they are based. In short, shops should be active wherever their customers are.

VIDEO SITES

Other social media sites are the video sites such as YouTube. Here video clips can be uploaded of brands, people or shops. YouTube is one of the most visited sites for information. A film, after all, says more than a thousand words. People are more visually oriented than textually. What's more, a video is a good medium for explaining a particular product, or giving an impression of the look and feel of a shop or providing a clear idea of certain developments. This video can be uploaded onto the company's own site with a link to YouTube. It is also possible to upload the video directly onto YouTube. In much the same way, brands can build an image or shops create traffic. Just have a look on YouTube for videos of shops such as Abercrombie and Fitch or Harrods of London. Many other brands can also be found, including the striking videos of Evian. The video can be as expensive as you wish. You can also make videos with your own camera and simply upload them onto YouTube (with a link on your own website). Social media form new developments based on the Internet whereby like-minded people can find one another and communicate with one another about subjects that interest them. This can be through short texts such as on Twitter, via blogs or images (photos and videos). Communities can also be formed where groups can inform one another and share their opinions and thoughts. This is certainly a development that can be significant for brands, shops and shopping centres. Just take a look at the video about the Trafford Centre.

eBay/Gumtree: Classified Ad Sites

These so-called classified ad sites bring buyers and sellers together. Someone who has something to sell posts an ad on the website, and someone wishing to buy looks at the offers on the site and then perhaps makes an offer. A simple principle, which actually goes back to the origins of trade. Visitors to the sites intend to buy, so why not bring their attention immediately to new products or shops? This can be done through a fixed advertisement next to a product group or specific article, or by linking the company website to an article in a fixed place (embedded). This is a good medium for online retailers to attract customers to their webshop, as well as for physical retailers to get customers into their shops. A referral to the shop can be made thanks to the possibility of linking the offer to a postcode, as well as the possibility of a *local login*, whereby only those offers of local suppliers are shown. Smaller businesses are thereby also able to offer their services, such as a domestic help living locally, a nearby private individual selling a second-hand car or a local garage selling new and second-hand cars.

Due to the wide range of products offered on such classified ad sites, it is this very locally oriented availability of products that is so interesting for attracting customers to the shop. Visitors to the site are looking to buy anyway and would be happy to buy something in the area, where they can see it, test it and take it home with them straightaway. Local shops should therefore develop a strategy for these classified ad sites as well as for the local sites such as those of the local councils. In addition, it is also possible to place referrals to one another to direct customers to each other's shop or product offers (affiliate).

Affiliates

An affiliate is an old form of providing a referral to one another's shop or product offers as described earlier. This used to take place in the shop, and later through joint special offers or joint advertising (co-advertising). These days this mainly takes place online. With affiliates there is a referring site (the affiliate) and a business or webshop. The referring site refers the visitors to the shop. This is sometimes done on the basis of products such as we have seen with the classified ad sites, and sometimes via an app or someone else's website. With an app of a city or local council you can search according to shop or product, which then refers you to the nearest location. Particularly in the near future, when the penetration levels of smartphones and tablets will have increased considerably, this will be an important element in attracting new customers. Through these apps, special offers can be made to visitors of a city or shopping centre (*location based* or *near field communication*) or via the particular website (push via LBS or pull via apps).

An affiliate concept is also collaboration between suppliers and can go much further than just a referral. A network can be created by carrying out active referrals. This would, however, have to be suppliers that fit in with the buying pattern and the buying association of the customer. Consider, for example, the recommendation of a certain suit by a shoe shop, or the recommendation of shoes by a men's clothes shop, as well as a discount on a lunch or coffee with cake or the offer of car parking. If it seems to make sense for a customer, then it provides a benefit. It is the personal identification that is provided by a card (such as the London's Oyster travel card) or smartphone that makes it possible to send a 'coupon' that can be read by another supplier, even if it is just a bar code by telephone. There will also be concepts for an 'electronic wallet'. This possibility will be integrated within an existing chip on the telephone or a generic card. This makes it possible to manage virtual (or real) money. This virtual money can then be used in another shop or with another supplier. Key to this application is that customers are referred in a particular associated network, and can see the logic in this as well as the benefits. This can be used in a shopping centre or shopping streets based on association and needs, for tourism services for example. A local zoo, restaurants and cafes can be included. Tourist destinations may include a cycle route that refers cyclists to local facilities, such as shops, cafes and restaurants along the route. This could also include extra information via the tablet or smartphone if you are in the vicinity of a particular place of interest (*location based services*).

Cloud Computing

The term *cloud computing* refers to data being available via the Internet everywhere and at any time. Simply by logging in you have access to your data. Google, in particular, is a strong partner in the cloud. Through Hotmail and Gmail you can access your email on any computer, and on Prezi.com you can, for example, show your presentations at any time using any computer. Logging in with the correct password provides constant access to your data. It is conceivable that in this way the mobile phone will allow people access to a specific cloud that could be activated when they go shopping (via an app). The shopkeeper would then always be able to see what visitors have done on the Internet, what their preferences are and perhaps also their buying intentions. By automatically reading their cloud, specific messages could be sent to them or they would be able to check specific information themselves. This is handy when, for example, people suffer from a particular allergy or are looking for dietary products. It would allow them to check straightaway whether such a product meets the necessary criteria. By scanning the article with a mobile phone, product ingredients could be compared against their allergy specification, and they would then know whether they can eat that particular food. The cloud of the shop/the product contains information on the ingredients, but also associated products. A person's own cloud has information on the allergy. The two clouds then compare the data and assess whether it is wise to make the purchase.[3] The applications of clouds are still somewhat limited at the moment; they are currently only used on application level. It is, nevertheless, expected that this application will become an important infrastructure in the future, whereby the smartphone and tablets will form an important basis for access. Because of this, it is possible for a customer to no longer shop anonymously and for a retailer to respond directly to a customer, based on information and historical behaviour.

---

3   For and example of this see http://www.techterms.com.

Payment Systems

Another development that has been driven by technology is the payment methods at the end of the sales process. The traditional model involved paying in cash. Later, direct debit cards were introduced, whereby the money would be transferred directly into the bank account of the company. Credit cards are often also a possible payment method, whereby the payment to the retailer does not take place straightaway, but via a debt collection procedure with the cardholder after which the money is transferred to the retailer. The costs of the various payment forms can vary quite substantially. Paying by cash requires certain transactions such as collecting the money and taking it to the bank. When paying with a direct debit card using a pin number, the payments go straight to the bank and costs a few cents or pennies. With credit cards commission is paid to the credit card company, usually based on a few per cent. The Internet provides the same possibilities as a physical shop. Customers can pay by credit card, a cheque or cash on delivery. All these forms of payment are variants of direct cash payments. The major innovation is in fact paying direct by Internet like Google wallet or Paypal. These new ways of paying in the shop and on Internet has advantages for the customer (ease of use) and the retailers (security). On top of this, the traditional forms of payment were vulnerable to fraud: cash on delivery relied on customers paying as agreed only after the company had gone to the trouble of delivering the item, cheques led to companies waiting for customers finally sending off the cheques and credit cards were vulnerable to hacking. The necessity for a new form of payment led to new alternatives being offered. Further developments will particularly come from the possibility of paying using the mobile phone. It is possible to install an RFID chip in the mobile phone to allow contact-free payments at the checkout, but an app on the phone is also a possibility. New entrants to payment platforms, such as telecom companies, will certainly stimulate these new forms of payment.

Loyalty

It is then up to the loyalty of the customers whether or not shops have a future. Loyalty is a conscious decision; customers have to be motivated to buy and to return to the shop. It is therefore a shame to see that the majority of loyalty programmes are in fact discount programmes. Whether it is collecting stamps or registering a customer's purchases, it does not matter which, they all lead to a discount. But if customers really wanted a discount and save money, wouldn't they simply go to the cheapest supplier? Then they really would get the cheapest deal. Furthermore, these so-called loyalty programmes do not really lead to loyalty, but simply to conscious purchasing. After all, generating turnover is important, but what is the real objective? A good loyalty programme responds to the needs of customers and the desired bond with them. Association with a particular brand, being able to identify with a group of users or with an image, these are all (social) bonding factors. The reduction of uncertainty can sometimes also be an important factor. If a person is uncertain, he tends to buy from a well-known brand rather than from an unknown brand. People visiting, for example, India or Pakistan would tend to buy Pepsi or Coca-Cola rather than the local brand: loyalty through uncertainty. There are also various forms of structural bonding. The subscription with telecom companies, the Internet subscription, maintenance and warranty contracts are all examples of these. Also those retailers who succeed in stimulating customers to return have managed to create a structural bond. A typical example is the structural bond with your dentist. Driven by anxiety, habit or simply the 'historical' record, patients keep on returning to the same dentist. Even when they have moved house they are reluctant to change, as this structural bond is very strong. A discount programme rewards transactions, the purchases. The bonding factor here is the discount. Although this has worked well in the past, the question is whether this will continue to do so in the future. Customers are becoming increasingly comfortable with buying from other shops, on the Internet or through special deals. This all reduces the sense of loyalty, and, as a result, financial stimuli only have a short-term effect. Typical examples of this are the daily special offers of shops and the Internet that are only available for that one day. The special deals sites such as Groupon, Social living, Vente-Exclusive and Google also profit from this.

There are possibilities in physical shops as well. IKEA has for years had information terminals for the family club showing special offers and interesting deals, and supermarkets such as Tesco show special offers based on a customer's historical buying behaviour. Both concepts are supported with email communication. These sorts of possibilities still offer plenty of opportunities, via an information terminal which reads a customer card or automatically via Near Field Communication or applications on the cloud. These allow for direct recognition in the shop, which results in direct communication on special offers, suggestions for purchases or other interesting deals. Customers have to be continually surprised and motivated in order to stimulate a preference to buy. The process of selling, which is still very much product and transaction-oriented, must transform into a process that is based on needs and desires. Technology can help in this, whereby getting to know the behaviour of customers must form the basis. But we can also keep it simple; the shop must take on the role of host and make customers feel welcome. The Americans, Japanese and, in Europe, the Germans already do this quite well.

Cheap Shops and 'Flash Shop', the Answer to Technology?

We will also see increasingly more flash concepts being employed in shopping streets. Due to the increasing numbers of empty properties along the high street, owners will be more willing to enter into short-term rental contracts. This allows for no-nonsense concepts: no expensive inventory or systems and no loyalty programmes, simply low prices and payment in cash. *Outlet stores, dump stores* or *boot sales* in the shop. Here today, gone tomorrow.

> *99p Stores sell 10,000 types of product, 70% of which are well-known brands such as Colgate and Mars. The company buys the products in large quantities and often in countries where they are cheaper such as Greece and the Netherlands. Recently, a start was also made on selling foods such as 99p sandwiches and meat products.*
>
> *Faisal Lalani, purchasing director: 'Initially we looked for areas with low income groups but a high density population such as Holloway in London. But when Woolworths closed we also started to test locations in areas that were a little more up-market, cities such as Lymington and Stroud. We soon realised that these people, too, were looking to buy bargains. Initially, the local councils were rather negative about our arrival, a little snooty, and wanted to determine precisely who was and was not allowed to set up a shop. But these are now two of our most successful shops. Those people who are a little better off also spend a little bit more!'*

In Spain, Chinese shops have brought local shopkeepers into difficulties. In areas where a decade ago local shopkeepers were prominent features on the high streets and beginning to profit from the upturn in tourism, they have now almost been completely wiped out by Chinese shops. These shops have now flooded the Costas, offering a wide range of articles at unprecedentedly low prices. The quality may not be that good, but as the prices are sometimes 10% of those of the regular local shops, customers can afford to buy a new one when necessary. In other words, why should tourists take bags full of clothes to the Costa with them when they can buy them so cheaply over there?

Leaving the products behind is therefore no longer an option, but a logical consequence. Wallmart has had the same effect in many cities in America, and Primark will undoubtedly also have the same impact in the cities wherever they set up shops. In England the 99p stores are becoming increasingly popular. Everything costs 99p. Initially, shop premises were sought in neighbourhoods with people on low incomes living in mainly rented accommodation, but much to the owners' surprise the success of this concept was not limited to just these neighbourhoods. People in areas with medium incomes and higher were also attracted to these cheap shops. They attract the same public as Primark; a higher social class does not mean to say that you are averse to discounts. This is also the case with the Chinese shops in Spain and the *flash stores* and *outlet stores*. The IKEA concept is similar to this, and has won over customers from other home furnishing companies.

Plenty of purchasing and experiences, all at reasonably low prices; it seems like a response to the Internet and the technology. Bulk sales in shops that are sometimes permanent and temporary use of empty shop premises are becoming increasingly popular amongst consumers. Other shops concentrate on fighting for the customer's loyalty, in order to ensure continuity, by motivating customers in the old-fashioned way: experience, surprises and customer knowledge. Technology will play an important role in this; the retail sector has to look closely at new, modern loyalty concepts again. Purchases can be recorded at the checkout and then, based on the customer's location and buying behaviour, customised special offers should be made for the customers via the Internet. Not only are the customers attracted to the shop in this way, but they are also introduced to the retailer's website, making it very easy to buy something straightaway. This is a form of cross-retailing with a chain of shops where loyalty for anything other than price is not immediately obvious.

Retail in the Future, Technology Driven

Technology will have a significant impact on the retail sector. Technology supports the core process, but will also increasingly support the buying process. The so-called *Tweet mirrors* already make it possible to take a photo of your reflection and send this directly to Twitter or the email addresses of your friends. Webcams make it possible to show you live what you look like, whilst image projects will enable you to project your personal preferences and image. This is an integral application of data from the client combined with a new methodology of reflection, and allows Internet applications to be integrated within the physical shop.

> *Nola Donato, from Intel Labs, the computer chip manufacturer which is developing the system, said: 'It means that shoppers can get an answer to practical questions such as whether their bum looks big in something without even having to set foot in the shop. This can be both in the mirror and also via a reflection on the shop window. You don't even have to go into the shop to try out an item of clothing!'*

> *'We can produce a three-dimensional model of a dress and put it on the body on screen to allow customers to see how they would look in that item. They would be able to mix and match, or try different sizes to see if it looks different. We are also working on how to make the clothing look and move realistically to give the best possible idea of how an item would look on the customer. Synchronisation ensures that the image no longer looks like a clumsy moving mannequin but a real life image.'*

Source: http://www.telegraph.co.uk/technology/news/8583823

As a result of the application of technology, the Internet and the physical shop are growing closer to one another. The technology, however, is no longer merely aimed at supporting the retail process, but on supporting the customers. Examples include iPad consoles next to products, such as what Apple has done, or in-store terminals like House of Fraser has done in, the *Tweet mirror* used in the WE chain of clothes shops, and purchasing support with online shopping lists as provided by the Dutch retail chain Albert Hein. New technological possibilities are becoming available within the physical world increasingly often, enabling the Internet and the physical shops to grow towards one another. So we see the shop on the Internet providing information and communication, but also the Internet in the shop providing information and sales support. For both these applications the data has to be stored so that the customer can be recognised immediately, both on the Internet and in the shop. This is possible by using the same database with the same customer identification. Not only does physical shopping have to become more fun, but it also has to be better supported with technology that enables customer recognition in the shop and allows support to be given through videos and information. This development, however, is not unique to the retail trade. These days cars also incorporate much more technology than they used to do. They provide extensive information on the dashboard, and often have a navigation and a parking system. These applications have nothing to do with the car engine itself, but only help to improve the driving comfort as well as assist the driver in driving more quickly and safely. Advanced technology is also commonplace at the office. An office without a computer is unthinkable, and an analysis of a football game is no longer conceivable without technology. So the retail sector is certainly not leading the way when it comes to adopting the latest technology. This new technology can, however, help in responding to the latest developments faced by the retail sector. Technology has a facilitative function, and its application is moving from the back office to the shop and then ultimately to the buying process; in other words, a movement towards the customer. This movement is identical to what is usually seen in the application of technology: from efficiency, to effectiveness and then to integration. If, in this way, the retail sector is open to the new applications and opportunities of technology, whereby the Internet-related applications will lead the way, then there is a future. Then the old values can once more play a prominent role, but in another manner; supportive, customer-friendly, service-oriented and welcoming, but particularly with the objective of creating a motivated, loyal customer. That's what retail was all about and that's the way it will stay. The retail concept, however, has to be placed in the present and based on the buying behaviour of today *and* tomorrow.

Conclusion and Summary of Chapter 5

Table 5.1   Impact of development and technology on the retail sector

Traditional	Development	New/future	Technology
Trade margin	Declining due to new distribution channels, other relationship with suppliers and breakdown of supply chain.	Strong relationship through embedded propositions and collaboration in NFC, and communication towards customers .	Embedded software on the company's webshop, terminals and NFC in the shop, automatic ordering, VMI, supply chain concepts with greater manufacturer/supplier risk. Tracking and tracing and direct communication towards end-users.
Property	Declining due to other concept of shopping centres (rent) and reducing the value of shopping centres and commercial property.	Concentration on 'magnet locations' such as old city centres, old cities and local attractions.	Compensation for costs of property at important locations by suppliers. Closer collaboration from production to sales. Solidarity (bearing risks with the retail sector).

Table 5.1   Continued

Traditional	Development	New/future	Technology
Interest revenue.	Declining due to a different buying behaviour and new payment systems.	New prepaid systems. Subscription forms with another proposition, no longer price per product but price per customer or per period.	Collaboration with financial service providers for new payment concepts, payment instalment systems.
Transaction profits	Declining due to increased competition and the Internet.	Part of an integrated concept as a result of which product margin is compensated by other services (or up-selling).	Greater margin through services. Core product is low margin, profit on other activities (affiliates) and services. Also use new business concepts to determine what customers want to pay for, and what price (see Ryanair concept).

6

New Concepts, New Opportunities: You Can't Change the Past, but You Can Change the Future!

The Changes in the Market

The old value components of the retail sector have become weaker. This is not only due to the different behaviour of customers, but also because of a variety of developments such as internationalisation, large powerful brands, the application of technology and government policy. It simply means that because of the resulting change in market conditions, the strengths and weaknesses have to be re-examined through a sort of self-reflection. What are the opportunities and what are the threats? The classic approach of the SWOT analysis assumes that the conditions and structures from which the opportunities and threats can be deduced are constant. Porter's competition model (with its five forces) shows the various influences on the market, based on the market's current structure. The model incorporates substitutes, entrants and the *value chain*.

Implicit in this model is that the market conditions can change, which in turn can lead to new structures. And this is exactly what is happening now in the retail trade. Due to external causes, such as those described above, the market conditions are changing as well as the structure of the market. Retailers therefore have to assess once more how to respond to this. Do the same thing but better? Do the same more cheaply? Do something different or determine the principles once again and then draw conclusions from this? There are various causes for the changes: the new shopping, the different buying behaviour of customers, the new entrants and the ease of buying abroad on the Internet or at shops (see Top Shop, John Lewis, Marks & Spencer and Primark, but also Amazon.com). There are also the (brand) manufacturers, who sell directly or open up their own flagstores, as well as the substitute possibilities such as the Internet and *flash stores*. Is shopping a necessity or a leisure activity? Isn't shopping also a day out? As far as the technology is concerned, mobile Internet in particular will lead to major changes in the shopping behaviour. Take, for example, the connection of shops with *location-based services*: Places, Foursquare and the use of Facebook (or Google+). The physical component is once more *connected*; customers are informed and guided, but can gain access to all the desired information and contacts. This development is still in its infancy but will act as a catalyst for the changes. Mobile Internet will become more important in the future. With a mobile device a customer can check prices and availability on the net (with competitors), but can also order direct while shopping.

THE MOBILE BARGAIN HUNTER

Black Friday witnessed the arrival of the mobile deal seeker who embraced their devices as a research tool for in-store and online bargains. Mobile traffic increased to 14.3 percent on Black Friday 2011 compared to 5.6 percent in 2010.

Mobile Sales: *Sales on mobile devices surged to 9.8 percent from 3.2 percent year over year.*

The Apple Shopper: *Mobile shopping was led by Apple, with the iPhone and iPad ranking one and two for consumers shopping on mobile devices (5.4 percent and 4.8 percent respectively). Android came in third at 4.1 percent. Collectively iPhone and iPad accounted for 10.2 percent of all online retail traffic on Black Friday.*

The iPad Factor: *Shoppers using the iPad led to more retail purchases more often per visit than other mobile devices with conversion rates reaching 4.6 percent compared to 2.8 percent for overall mobile devices.*

Surgical Shopping Goes Mobile: *Mobile shoppers demonstrated a laser focus that surpassed that of other online shoppers with a 41.3 percent bounce rate on mobile devices versus online shopping rates of 33.1 percent.*

Source: IBM.com, 26 November 2011.

A Battle for the Customer

The battle for the customer in the future will be fought on the Internet. The impending challenge for retailers will be to motivate the customer to buy. Retailers can meet this challenge on their own, but also in partnership with other retailers or with the supplier. This does mean, however, that there has to be a mutual interest for all parties and that it should lead to benefits for the customer. Retailers will have to take a fresh look at their business model and re-examine where costs are incurred and where money can be made. In the future, it will no longer be tenable to rely upon a transaction-based business model, focused on sales transactions. A business model that is based on transaction profit is not directed at the business contacts and customers, and is certainly not customer friendly. It focuses only on making profit from sales. And it is precisely this strategy that is under pressure due to the current developments. For decades, companies have been working in this transaction-oriented manner; change will therefore not be easy. Yet it will be necessary in order to survive. Of all the business models, the transaction-based model is perhaps the simplest one. However, it is a model where the retail trade runs all the risks and no room is given for a consistent strategy based on the customer. 'Sell, pay and then next customer please. Exchanging the purchase is a bit of a bother, so preferably not.' Do retailers really think that the customer is happy with this and will come back? In the rest of this chapter I will examine other business models that provide a better foundation for the future.

New Business Models

TRADITIONAL TRANSACTION-DRIVEN RETAIL MODEL

It is of course not surprising that in a transaction-driven model, such as the one that is actually still being used in the retail sector, with its strong focus on products, it is the product properties that are central. Also in marketing the marketing instruments are used for acquiring a good position. Product, place, promotion and price, supplemented in the retail trade by personnel, are good instruments within a sales paradigm for determining the proposition. But this approach ignores the essence. Before a shop was opened up and a product was developed, sound research was carried out into the need for it. Based on the needs of the consumers or companies, a product was developed that met these identified needs. The product was then presented and positioned by using these instruments (the four Ps) in the appropriate manner. After this, however, only the product properties or imaginary properties of the product were communicated. It was forgotten that the product was bought in order to meet a need. If the need changes, then the product will have to change as well or a new solution will have to be offered, regardless of how good the original product is. The same applies to the shop. A shop is set up after carrying out sound market research or based on past experiences. If the historical criteria change, it is obvious that it will be necessary to reassess whether the shop still meets a particular need. Perhaps this is no longer the case or perhaps the shop has to be changed according to the new circumstances. And that is exactly what is happening at the moment. The market circumstances have changed due to the development of the Internet and the new buying behaviour. It is therefore logical for the retail sector to think seriously about the benefits and value it can provide.

But it is not only the market circumstances that have changed. The very essence of trade has come under pressure. Trade developed in order to overcome the constraints of time, place and quantity. That is why we are able to eat oranges and drink coffee the whole year round, despite there being just a single harvest, somewhere far away. But what if this propulsion of products in the *supply chain* is no longer necessary? If consumers can buy directly from a manufacturer, then links in the *supply chain* will be eliminated. This applies to wholesalers, distributors and in some cases also to the traditional retailers. These days the technology, which includes direct links, tracking and tracing and efficient international transport, allows for other, shorter and more direct structures. And the old model, in which the retail sector bore so much risk, is not ready for the future. After all, why should the retailer run so much risk, while the manufacturer runs very little or even no risk at all? The fashion industry in particular is coming under pressure from the Internet, webshops and the recession. A number of years ago, some clever webshops bought up surplus stocks with discounts sometimes as high as 70%. The manufacturer had overproduced and had to get rid of some of his stocks before the new season started. Physical retailers had signed for orders, sometimes six months prior to the start of the season and still had to get rid of their existing stocks. These surplus stocks were then offered by webshops at reduced prices, which understandably led to irritation amongst the retailers with physical shops. The stocks were also offered at the standard prices but an aggressive sales strategy was followed, resulting in some very attractive margins. As this led to a great deal of tension in the sales channel, manufacturers decided to work no longer with two seasons per year and to reduce the risk of surplus stocks. Instead, they decided to work with more seasons. These days the major labels add a new collection to their range every month. This allows for smaller quantities to be made, thereby minimising the risk of surplus stocks. What's more, by using new information and production techniques, it is possible to respond to changes in the demand very quickly. ZARA and Top Shop, for example, surprise their customers with new products each week. Thanks to the small production numbers, manufacturers do not run any risks. The customers, too, benefit from this. These articles have a high stock turnover rate and can be offered at very competitive prices. This stimulates customers to buy more and more frequently. It also stimulates customers to come into the shop more often to see what is new, to hopefully find new clothes. This has been a successful response to the conflict in the channel, the potential threat of the Internet through low prices and the new buying behaviour.

The stock risk in the fashion industry has traditionally been almost entirely borne by the retailers. The suppliers produce only what the retailers had signed for in the pre-buying. The risk of not selling all the stocks to the consumer thereby lay squarely on the shoulders of the retailer.

Increasingly more suppliers realise that this approach in the current market was too short-sighted. You can only really speak of a successful collection if all the articles were actually bought by the consumer at the normal sales price and if there has been a high turnover rate. If not, then the retailer will invariably suffer a margin loss as a result of markdowns, which will adversely affect the profits of the retailer. This will eventually impact the supplier in the next purchasing round when the retailer is left with a lower purchasing budget, regardless of the quality of the collection. The cycle of this phenomenon can only be broken if the supplier feels involved in the sales result of his collection on the shop floor.

Successful Businesses Go Further

Suppliers not only show involvement but also share some responsibility. This is the chain reversal trend. Many successful concepts are now more supplier driven than retail driven. The verticals and the monobrand shops of A-brands are well-known examples of this. But also in the multibrand environment we increasingly come across supplier-driven business models, such as Vendor Managed Inventory (VMI), Concession and Consignment. What characterises this is that the supplier takes care of the collection and the planning of the goods and that the retailer no longer places orders.

Source: Fashionunitedindicia.nl

FROM PUSH TO PULL, THE CUSTOMER IS SUPPLIER

The role of the consumer is also changing; it has moved up from the last link in the chain to the first link; a change from push to pull. The consumer now goes looking for what he regards as the best product. He specifies his wishes very accurately and then looks for a solution. In the simplest form he may state his wishes online on allowing suppliers to respond so that he can select the best party. Other examples include sites where you can place a description of what you are looking for, to which registered suppliers can respond. The customer then selects the best offer. Many more of these sites will undoubtedly emerge, whereby offers can be made in response to the wishes of businesses or consumers as end-users. The end-user therefore no longer has to look for the offer that best meets his wishes. Rather, suppliers will respond directly to the end-user's problem or wishes. Within the social media it is also becoming increasingly easy to first specify your wishes and then ask suppliers to make an appropriate offer. This is a complete reversal of the traditional model: suppliers looking for customers instead of customers looking for suppliers – a clear development of the pull process.

Variations of this are also possible within the traditional push process, such as joint purchasing. Place an offer on the Internet, stating that it will be sold once there are, for example, 100 potential buyers, and then just wait (the principle of *social shopping* as can be seen with Groupon and others). You can also have customers register for a certain product proposition. Once there are sufficient participants, the product can be manufactured. We already see this principle in the housing market. Once sufficient houses have been sold, the construction work for the project can commence. Considering the current slump in the housing market, it would not be surprising if this approach were to be taken again. We have seen this more frequently in the business-to-business market. Software manufacturers, for example, who looked for a *launching customer*. The program was first developed together with the customer (co-makership) and then launched onto the market. The first customer received a premium with further sales, a payback principle. This principle reduces the risks for the manufacturer, and the first customer can fulfil many of his wishes, giving the software package a pseudo-customised look. What's more, if it is successful in the market, the first customer will also benefit. This approach requires direct contact between the manufacturer and the user (customer), and does not in fact accommodate a role for an intermediary. The Internet links the two parties directly.

These changes lead to other market structures as well as to another role for the current parties such as shops. But every change also brings along opportunities, as long as you make the most of them. An example of this is AutoStyle.

REVERSED SUPPLY CHAIN MODEL

Another model is based on the retailer no longer having to bear the price risks on his own. It is in the interest of manufacturers as well that the retailer is successful and sells a great many products. One way of meeting the retailer halfway is the VMI model (vendor manages inventories) described earlier. In this model it is the supplier who bears the responsibility of the stocks held by the retailer. Together they make an agreement as to who has ownership of the stocks and when payments are to be made. In certain cases payment is made only once the product is sold, a sort of consignment model, but now the supplier is also responsible for the management of the stocks. The supplier replenishes the stocks, looks at what sells well and stimulates the sales through sound stock control. Another possibility is that the retailer is fully responsible for his shop, attracts visitors to the shop, provides a pleasant shopping environment and employs skilled staff. In short, he ensures there is a good shopping experience. The stock is then the responsibility of suppliers who also finance the stocks. This approach is particularly good for brand manufacturers as they will be able to not only have optimum control over the brand, but also work the market and offer the appropriate product range. As the manufacturers finance the stocks themselves, different agreements are made with the retailers and separate agreements are made regarding the mutual responsibilities. In this case we see a chain reversal. The starting point is the sales outlet, the moment that the customer considers to buy something. This involves a pull strategy which provides an ideal situation for the retailers to concentrate on a pleasant buying environment and for the manufacturer in turn on a good product and good brand experience.

CUSTOMER IN DIRECT CONTACT WITH THE IMPORTER/ MANUFACTURER (COLLABORATION STRATEGY)

AutoStyle[1] is an importer of car accessories and sells its products through selected dealers. The products are offered in a catalogue that dealers buy. We frequently see the same sort of principle in the retail sector where shops of, for example, home furnishing chains buy the sample books from the manufacturer. This selling strategy is part of the current business model. AutoStyle now offers

---

1   Autostyle is a concept of Autosport Tepper B.V. Interview with Dolf Kuiper, vice director of Twinkle.

these products online, and will probably eventually be able to do away with these books. Dealers can look up the product range as well as the relevant prices 24/7 online. Customers and dealers can buy the articles in the shop. If they are in stock, they can be taken home straight away; if not, they can quickly be sent from a central warehouse to the dealer. The customer contact goes through the dealer, who delivers the article, gives advice and if necessary even installs it. As we have seen, the market is changing; the dealer is no longer the delivery point, but has now become a service point. Customers can go to the dealer in the traditional manner, but they can also buy online at home where they can select a local dealer. Based on a postcode or login point, a local dealer is suggested. The chosen dealer will then be the service point and will maintain contacts with the customer. The customer can choose between having the items delivered at home or collecting them from the chosen service point (*click and collect*). If the customer has any questions, he goes to the service point. The further communication, such as special offers, emails or newsletters, will always be carried out on behalf of the dealer. No conflicts will arise in the channel as this service is provided in order to support the dealer.

COLLABORATION WITH MANUFACTURERS

This application is based on a close collaboration between the manufacturer/ importer and the dealer or retailer. This collaboration is also possible by providing extra support in the shop to customers through, for example, installing interactive screens or information terminals next to the products. This can support the buying process, particularly if the products require further explanation. In the case of a fashion shop this may show fashion videos; with an electronics shop this could be, for example, videos describing the use of computers, and in the case of do-it-yourself shops information regarding installation, use of the product or ordering possibilities. Particularly for products that cannot be taken home straight away, ordering is an option, as a home delivery would have to be arranged. The manufacturer takes care of the infrastructure and possibly also the delivery to the customer, but this would have to be on behalf of the retailer. An intermediate form is to use a logistics company such as Katoen Natie in Antwerp Belgium, a gateway for Europe for many suppliers. Katoen Natie can supply the retailers with the stocks on behalf of the manufacturers but can also deliver directly to customers' homes on their behalf. The ordering is carried out by either the retailer or the customer, whilst the stocks are kept with Katoen Natie in Antwerp and the chosen transport company delivers the order to the shop (the stocks of the shop are also delivered in this manner) or to the customer's home. It is essential that there is a close collaboration between manufacturer, Katoen Natie, retailer and the transport company.

Also with VMI we see a close collaboration between the retailer and supplier. There are clear agreements regarding positioning, sales support and stocks. One of the pioneers in this area was Sorbo, who as early as the 1980s put up display racks in supermarkets. The stock difference between two time periods therefore represented the sales. Sorbo bore the risks of the rack and the stocks. For retailers this was a good way of making a return from their available shop floor area without any form of risk. This same principle can still be successful within a sophisticated VMI concept. The ordering and payment can be carried out fully automatically. Trust and mutual interests are essential to this concept.

> *The Dutch company Sinner (sport glasses and sunglasses) makes displays available to multibrand retailers and manages these through a remote electronic data exchange system. This is not only for the basic models, but also for the more trendy glasses which therefore carry greater risks. Using the VVMI model, Sinner has managed to greatly increase its turnover which in turn has given retailers a considerably higher return per square metre. An additional benefit for this supply is that the Sinner brand has gained considerably more exposure on these external shop floors.*

> *Source*: Fashionunitedindicia.nl

MULTI-CHANNEL STRATEGY

Retailers have always been involved in selling, and so it is logical that they regard the Internet also as an opportunity to sell. In addition to the physical shop, retailers are looking to set up their own website to compensate for the decline in turnover due to the Internet. What is often forgotten, however, is that selling on the Internet is different from selling in the physical world. It starts with the name already; is the physical name also a logical one for the Internet? How do you acquire a top-of-mind position and how do you obtain added value on the Internet? Then there is the danger of price erosion or a lack of clarity among customers regarding differences in delivery conditions between the Internet and the physical world. The EU requires that webshops employ a 14-day return and exchange policy on articles. In physical shops, however, sometimes changing or returning an article is not allowed. If the webshop has a home shopping guarantee hallmark then it makes sense that the conditions in the physical shop are approximately the same. In addition, the Internet requires knowledge of customers, direct communication and interactivity. These are specific fields. In order to bypass these problems, businesses often opt for a multi-channel strategy whereby the Internet is a specific channel with its own proposition and often its own label!

MEDIAMARKT AND REDCOON UNDER THE SAME ROOF

The Media-Saturn Holding, parent company of MediaMarkt, is taking over Redcoon. As an independent subsidiary the international online retailer in consumer electronics will continue with its own commercial strategy. Rumours have already been circulating about this takeover.

Only Online

It is not known how much was paid for Redcoon. Once approved by the competition authorities, Redcoon will be active on the market under the wings of Media-Saturn. Within the group, however, Redcoon will remain active in the online segment only. The company will retain its head office in Aschaffenburg. Reiner Heckel stays on as general director and partner of the independent subsidiary of the Media-Saturn Group, which will compete with MediaMarkt and Saturn. MediaMarkt has for some time now been experimenting with a webshop that has not really managed to take off.

Strategy

'The company fits in very well with the Media-Saturn portfolio', says Dr Rolf Hagemann, CFO of the Media-Saturn Holding GmbH, vice chairman of the board and responsible for Mergers & Acquisitions:

> With the acquisition we will gain access to the e-commerce activities in Germany and nine other European countries. The business is already established and is a reliable player in the area of e-commerce. As of now we'll expand the online activities of our MediaMarkt and Saturn brands as an independent unit. Redcoon is therefore an essential part of our online strategy.

402 Million euros

Redcoon, which was set up by a former MediaMarkt employee in 2003 in the German city of Aschaffenburg, has since developed into a major player in the online sale of consumer electrical goods. The webshop is active in 10 European countries, and employs 485 staff. The expected turnover for the financial year not coinciding with the calendar year 2010/2011 is 402 million euros.

Source: Twinklemagazine.nl, 31 March 2011.

MediaMarkt is an emotion shop and, due to the type of products it sells, attracts mainly men. Being able to see and touch the products as well as talk about them makes men keen to possess them. The long opening hours, often from 9a.m. to 9p.m., and the perceived low prices are very appealing. MediaMarkt also plays well upon the feeling of the moment. The special offers often only apply at particular branches, but visitors don't know that until they are in the shop, and sometimes a special offer can be spontaneous. The products may be in the shop now, but perhaps in an hour they will return to the warehouse again. So visitors wouldn't want to miss the chance of a bargain by thinking about it, or comparing it first with another product or another shop where it may be cheaper. This creates a feeling of wanting to act straightaway before it's too late. Men in particular are quite emotional when it comes to electronics, and MediaMarkt responds to that. A strong presence on the Internet does not really fit in with this strategy. This would be at the expense of the local differences, the autonomy of the local management and the strategy of non-transparency. In order to win the attention of the consumer, and perhaps also specifically the female buyer, a separate label and a multi-channel strategy is the only solution. The takeover of Redcoon fits in perfectly with this strategy. The company's own business model for the shops can remain, and another management can try to attract the online customers as well. The conditions for a cross-channel strategy, as we saw before are not suitable for MediaMarkt. They have a dominant position in the physical and emotional world and their sales strategy is strongly transaction and moment-driven. The Internet would detract from this. In local shops the culture of a family business is still central, with an emphasis on involvement and support. The website is an extension of the shop, and the shop an extension of the Internet. This is an example of a multi-channel strategy whereby the channels mutually reinforce one another as well as strengthen the relationship with the supplier.

Characteristics of a successful multi-channel retailer:[2]

- They recognise the uniqueness of each channel.

---

2   Source: www.retailonlineintegration.com, 16 October 2010. W. Klaassen, Online direct sales, 2010, MBA thesis, p. 25.

- They plan, which is crucial from the business plan up to the communication.

- They regularly re-evaluate each plan.

- They consolidate all sales across the channels. This provides greater negotiation power to suppliers.

- They provide a consistent customer experience across all the channels: from *look and feel* to the product range all the way to shopping convenience.

In all cases, these companies respond to the market developments in their own way and approach them on the basis of their own particular strengths: MediaMarkt with emotion and price perception and local shops with service and involvement. The electronics sector is certainly leading the way when it comes to change.

People who buy electronics naturally have a great affinity with innovations and technology and initially comprised a younger buying public. The book and music industries were the first sectors that noticed the effects of the different buying behaviour, and they are still looking for the right response. The book trade has not yet found an answer to this change. It would make sense if the book product were to be adapted to the new possibilities of the technology first, the essence of the book (reading, recreation, knowledge or entertainment) and the integration with the Internet, online information and videos within the 'book product'. From that moment other concepts would be conceivable, such as service and subscription concepts based on databases or new applications (video releases). The book as a *stand-alone* physical product will make room for an integrated product. Booksellers now have to be creative with their own business model. But this challenge also applies to many other industries, such as for toys, estate agents and project developers.

THE CUSTOMER-ORIENTED STRATEGY

The customer-oriented strategy is a strategy that can best be carried out by the smaller shops – personal contact, good experience, responding to the wishes of the customers and providing service. It sounds so easy, but is in fact applied so infrequently. If the shopkeeper and in particular the personnel were only just a little bit more friendly and helpful, smiled once in a while and assumed the role of host, then a great deal would have been achieved already. Listening to customers also means learning from them, and that does not happen very often in the retail trade.

ZARA
The Reversed Business Model Begins with the Customer!

ZARA is a determined company with a frequently changing collection, attractive prices, little advertising and an unprecedented turnover growth (in 2010 increased by 13% to 12.53 billion with a profit growth of 32% to 1.73 billion euros). 5,000 shops in 77 countries are provided with a new collection two times per week, a unique logistics process, a delivery time in Europe of maximum 24 hours, outside Europe 36 hours, within three weeks of the design idea to a garment in the shop! But this is not where the true strength of ZARA lies, although this is impressive compared with other suppliers who take at least six months to get an idea into the shop. The real strength lies in recognising the true wishes of customers and communicating this directly to the right people in the organisation! 'Shop managers keep the district managers informed on a daily basis regarding what customers want, what they dress like, what they buy, and what the trends are in a particular neighbourhood or city. These district managers in turn report several times a week to the market specialists who work in close contact with the designers.'

A classic business model is managed top-down: design, product development, shop, customer. Here, this is completely reversed (the reversed supply chain): model, customer, shop, design, product development. Short communication lines and the ever-changing range surprising customers at every visit to the shop. Due to the lack of intensive advertising campaigns the customer does, however, have to come to the shop to see all the wonderful new clothes. The low prices stimulate the customers to frequently try on the new collections. In England customer visits the same shop on average four times per year (non-food) whereas with ZARA this is 17 times per year! So the customers come almost twice per month to see what there is new! The small numbers of a collection encourage the customer to make a speedy decision, as tomorrow the garments may already be gone.

Source: FDweekend, ZARA Triumphs with Reversed Business Model, 26 March 2011, p. 20.

The business model also has to be changed based on the customer-oriented strategy. A transaction-based approach does not fit in with this strategy. A *share of wallet* or total concepts would be much better. This could be, for example, a fixed price based on the assessed wishes or needs. You see such offers with telecom companies where you pay a fixed price for a maximum number of services. The companies continue to assess whether the form of subscription optimally fits the customer's need or use. If this is possible with telecom companies, then it should also be possible with other companies where a continuous relationship with the customer is involved or to which the customer returns on a regular basis. Why doesn't the hairdresser ask for a fixed price per year? Certainly when it comes to men it can more or less be predicted how often they will come back. And if they wanted to come back an extra time, this could be included in the subscription. Of course, a customised fixed-price for women is also possible. But why not for toys, fashion and garden maintenance? The suppliers of such products are so stuck within the confines of their transaction framework that they have lost all creativity. But it is here, within this creativity, that the chances for survival lie. Don't think in terms of passes or loyalty discounts. Rather, consider different subscription rates for services and standard products. Conducting business in a customer-oriented manner means making the customer the focal point and getting to know him or her. Technology is good at facilitating this. A customer with a transaction-based approach continues to make a decision whether or not to purchase, and therefore continues to decide whether or not to buy at the shop. With a concept this decision will only be made once a certain period of time has elapsed (automatic continuation provides a solution to this). You don't end a relationship just like that. Subscriptions are not cancelled that often, whilst customers may make a decision every week whether or not to buy a particular magazine. This is the case not only with magazines, but also with many other products and sectors. But retailers have to discover that profit can sometimes be gained from this and that sometimes one has to make certain concessions. A long-lasting customer relationship that is based on *lifetime value* is interesting for both shops and customers. It gives peace of mind and certainty, and encourages the retailer to do something extra to ensure this certainty of custom. This could be in the form of extra service, an additional gift or a discount.

It is also essential to reach the customers. The shopping route has always been important to shops. A visitor walks through the various sections of the shop while spontaneously coming across the various products on offer. What's more, being associated with a magnet function such as stadiums, cinemas or a large shops leads to greater accessibility. Webshops have a similar problem. Opening a webshop is not enough in itself. It has to attract customers, which is much more difficult. Physical shops in fact have it easier in this respect due to all the passers-by.

THE MODULAR STRATEGY

A modular strategy is the opposite of the above fixed-price strategy and is based on a customer-oriented concept. The application of this modular strategy is a direct consequence of the new buying behaviour. Products used to be offered integrally, but over the last few decades they have been increasingly split up into separate units. We see this with the holiday industry, where customers used to buy all-inclusive holiday packages. These days people increasingly often book their flight, hotel and rental car separately. It is particularly this breakdown of products (and buying moments) that provides opportunities for retailers. It is possible to vary the concepts and prices, and it can be determined from where the profit will be derived. Particularly services that can form a separate component of the proposition can provide a good basis for making profits. Examples include maintenance, guarantees, checks, first choice and the possibility to exchange. Due to this breakdown, it is often difficult to determine the final price and therefore difficult to make comparisons. Increasingly it is required that the customer is able to compare the total final price – for example when booking air tickets or when arranging contracts with a telecom provider. The prices also have to state taxes (such as VAT and airport taxes), any surcharges and delivery costs. This is, of course, the government's response in trying to combat the lack of transparency of the various suppliers. Making comparisons allows people to find the cheapest article or even negotiate about the price (an increasing phenomenon in the retail sector).

City of London commentators believe Thomas Cook has rested on its laurels, trading on its reputation and sticking for too long by its traditional business model of buying hotel rooms and aircraft seats in advance, and selling them as a package via travel agents and brochures. 'If you don't differentiate your product, you will be hit on price because of the transparency of the web,' says Peter Long, chief executive of Tui Travel. The company now books a third of its business online. It has been more effective in protecting profit margins by developing a more upmarket product range than Thomas Cook has. This includes 'holiday villages' – hotels with sport and entertainment for all ages.

Both Tui and Thomas Cook aim to whittle down sprawling bricks-and-mortar store estates as lease renewals come due. But banks are likely to demand far more radical retrenchment at Thomas Cook. 'There aren't many options left for Thomas Cook apart from dramatically shrinking the business,' says Karl Burns.

Changing lifestyles, globalisation and new technology have a habit of destroying consumer businesses backed by historic brands. Examples include the UK high street retailer Woolworths, which closed in 2009, and tableware company Waterford Wedgwood, which collapsed into administration in the same year.

Source: Jonathan Guthrie and Roger Blitz, *Financial Times*, 25 November 2011.

With the modular strategy there is a main product, on top of which extra facilities can be acquired. The main product is competitively priced; the profit is made on the modules. The increased transparency will lead to greater attention for the main product that will be perceived as inexpensive. It is the modules that are the profit makers, but customers choose them consciously. One could also just buy the main product. A computer can be offered at a fairly low price, but the (dedicated) software is quite expensive. This was IBM's strategy in the 1960s, 1970s and still even in the 1980s. IBM was the market leader in mainframe computers and initially also in the PC market. Computers were very affordable; a maintenance contract, however, had to be signed and new releases of the operating software had to be purchased regularly. This maintenance contract and the updates were quite pricey and it is where IBM made its profits. Customers could not do without them, otherwise they would run the risk of the maintenance being terminated. Neither could customers call upon other parties without the risk of invalidating the guarantee. This business model was very successful for IBM for many years.

Similar constructions were initially also introduced for personal computers. In addition to the PC you had to buy a separate Windows operating system. In fact, without Windows your PC would not work. Based on Windows, integrated applications were developed as well, such as Word and Explorer. This was in fact a tied purchase, although the buyers often did not realise it. Other suppliers were not able to develop the market for word processors or Internet browsers as these were protected by Microsoft. The Windows operating system that was necessary to use the PC had an automatic link to Microsoft's own programs. It was only when the EU forbade this sort of forced tying that it was possible to develop new products and so offer buyers a choice. The tied selling was interesting to Microsoft because the operating system was necessary and, in particular, because people paid for the extra programs. The question remains whether this was a poor proposition for customers.

These days this modular strategy is successfully employed by Ryanair. The basic product, the flight, is very attractively priced. Once that is booked, the customer chooses the extras, such as priority boarding and the amount of luggage that is to be taken onboard. When the flight is booked can also influence the price. Booking and paying for the flight early leads to a lower price. You may well get even lower prices with last-minute bookings, but there is always a risk that the flight will be fully booked. It is possible that this strategy will be implemented further in the future. This would mean that you would also have to pay for a particular seat in the aircraft. There are now even discussions regarding whether passengers should pay per kilo of body weight. In all these cases the decision is up to the customer. The pricing is no longer to do with the cost price and therefore a profit per transaction. As customers determine for themselves what they want, they can also determine what they're willing to pay for and as a result make customised purchases.

THE AFFILIATE STRATEGY

With the affiliate strategy there is a partnership whereby one party offers the services of the other and receives a remuneration for this. Ryanair, for example, recommends to its customers Hertz as their favourite car-hire company. Ryanair customers receive a discount if they rent a car from Hertz. Due to this discount, customers are more likely to rent a car from Hertz than any other company. Hertz then knows straightaway which customers have come via Ryanair and so can give Ryanair a commission for this. In the same way similar arrangements can be made with hotels, cafes, restaurants and other service providers. Other airline companies, such as Transavia, employ a similar strategy. With the larger companies the affiliates are often linked to the loyalty programme. By making use of the services of these affiliates you can also save for *air miles* from the airline company. The collaborating parties, of course, pay a certain amount to the relevant airline company. If the customers' needs are used as a basis affiliates can be found quite easily. Customers would experience this as a service, whilst the suppliers would regard this as a component of a business concept. This revenue may result in a decreased return on the core product, for example through reduced prices, whereby the core product (for example the airline ticket) in turn also becomes cheaper. The result is that this company will attract more customers, thereby making it even more attractive for other potential collaborating parties.

In addition to the focus on the customer's needs, based on the core product, this can also be approached in terms of associations. The customer is central to this and obvious associations in the buying process are examined. This can also work effectively in the physical shop by working together with other physical shops or by referring to an allied webshop. Collection points are a simple form of this. If a customer prefers to collect an article from a shop instead of having it delivered to the home, the article can be collected from other participating physical shops. This is interesting for shops in the same specialist area, as this would create an association amongst customers. For books purchased on the Internet these could be collected from, for example, a local Waterstones branch and Waterstones may be competing with one another, but for customers there is a different type of purchasing perception. Even though we see the same product (books), there is a different buyer profile. As a result, this can create mutual benefits for both the webshop and the physical shop, as well as, of course, for the customer who has chosen this option. The customer can pick up the book (if he so wishes), and this results in traffic for the shop and the possibility of additional purchases.

Customers show a preference for webshops that also have a physical shop. This increases the customer's sense of trust; if there are any problems, the customer would be able to go to the shop. This provides opportunities for physical shops; webshops are looking for a physical location where their products can also be sold. So why not collaborate with physical shops and employ a form of shop-in-a-shop principle by displaying some of the collection there? Payment then simply takes place at the checkout. The web retailer does not have to be present himself but can make use of a physical shop's infrastructure. This provides benefits for the web retailer, the physical retailer as well as the customers. The web retailer is responsible for the product range of the shop whilst the logistics are the responsibility of the physical shopkeeper. Just as we see webshops companies such as Amazon.com provide services for physical retailers to sell online, physical retailers offer services to webshops to enable them to also have a physical presence. This gives rise to a specific form of cross-retailing.

CROSS-RETAILING

With cross-retailing the retailer is active both on the Internet and in the physical world. And all sorts of connections are possible. The simplest one is a multi-channel strategy such as described above. Another possible strategy is one whereby the Internet is used as an information medium in order to direct sales to the shop. The webshop provides information such as the location, the product range and opening hours, and a possibility for email contact. The sales are not carried out on the Internet. For this you would have to go to the shop. Manufacturers, too, can follow this strategy for their dealers. In a dealer situation it is possible that the manufacturer/importer arranges the online sales for dealers. Dealers still sell through the shop, but there are also service points for the online sales. The customer ownership and customer contact remains the responsibility of the dealer. Another similar possibility is if suppliers have an icon or link on the site of a shop (embedded in the shopkeeper website). By clicking on this link, the customer is directly connected to a supplier, although he would not notice this himself. This is a good solution particularly for customised products. The manufacturer supports the buying process and ultimately provides a customer with the choice: collect in the shop or have it delivered to the house. In all these cases the customer does not realise that the entire process takes place on the website of the other supplier/manufacturer. Here, too, the margin goes to the shop, and the customer contact is carried out either by the retailer or under his responsibility. This is an example of *dropshipping*. The retailer or webshop will sell the article but the delivery will take place direct from the manufacturer. The retailer does not have to invest in stocks and can concentrate on the customers. The profit margin goes direct to the retailer (see the example of Miele).

If a decision is made not to sell online, but always in the shop, an agreement can be made between the manufacturer and the shops that they both provide information via the Internet (an embedded solution is recommended here as well). On the Internet the visitor would be referred to the shop for personal advice and perhaps a demonstration. For example, if you are to truly appreciate Bose audio equipment you really do have to hear the equipment first-hand. For that reason Bose provides information on the Internet, but always sells its products through the shops of the dealer. This creates a sense of trust in the channel, between the shop and the supplier. It is, of course, a logical approach as far as the customers are concerned, as audio equipment really needs to be *heard*.

Another form of cross-retailing is a combination of the shop with the Internet. Shops can create a strong bond with customers, whereas the Internet can enable extra services to be provided. The physical shop is limited by its physical size, whereas this is not a problem for an Internet supplier. We increasingly see the concept of *click and collect* or *buy and collect* being employed, whereby customers buy on the Internet but collect the article in the physical shop. With shops such as H&M and John Lewis a large percentage of articles sold on the Internet are collected in their shops. The advantage for the customer is, of course, that they do not have to stay at home in order to receive the delivered articles. Another advantage is that they are able to exchange the articles in the shop straightaway, or leave them there if after closer inspection they decide against the purchase. The advantage for the retailer is that this concept creates traffic. The customer collecting the article may decide to buy more once he is in the shop. This also alleviates the problem of returning articles, as the articles are already in the shop and therefore immediately available for other customers to buy. But there is one other major advantage. As customers buy on the Internet, the articles do not have to be stocked in the shop. This allows the shop stocks to be kept to a minimum, which in turn requires less investment. Chains will be able to open up smaller shops in residential areas, suburbs and villages. After all, due to the smaller investment and floor space that is required the minimum turnover necessary to be profitable would be lower as well. All articles, however, would be available via the Internet and then collected in the shop.

This leads to a new shopping concept where you have smaller local shops close to the customer, large shops in the large shopping centres and everything available on the Internet which can be bought via *click and collect* and then picked up from the local shop. This concept is used by, for example, the John Lewis department stores. It helps John Lewis to increase the number of shops in its chain of department stores, its local visibility as well as the customers' loyalty. In addition, Internet sales can greatly expand the product range.

Web retailers may conclude from this that customers are happy to collect the articles they buy and so set up collection points. This is, however, not central to this concept. The articles are collected from the shop in question because they can be tried on and changed if necessary, advice can be given and perhaps accessories bought. This is much more than just a collection point. This development fits in perfectly with the outlined new shopping landscape: smaller shops in the city centres, residential areas and villages, and large shops in out-of-town shopping centres. The type of shops will also be different. In a city centre you tend to find more fun shops, boutiques and fashion shops, whereas in villages and residential areas they would mainly be small practical shops or shops with a product range for your routine daily shopping.

CAPTIVE STRATEGY/PRISONER STRATEGY

With a captive strategy, also known as a 'prisoner strategy', a customer has a bond with certain products. In this strategy there is a main product as well as dependent products such as supplies that have to be bought from specific suppliers. Hewlett Packard and many other printer manufacturers employ this strategy for their printers and cartridges. The printers are attractively priced, but customers do have to buy the specific cartridges of this make of printer – other cartridges either do not fit or would invalidate the guarantee on the printer. A similar strategy was implemented by Douwe Egberts and Philips (co-maker strategy) for their Senseo coffee machines and the coffee pads. This strategy was followed by most of the coffee machine manufacturers, including Nespresso. The machine works best with its own coffee pads or cups. The pads and cups are made to be unique for the machine (as with the cartridges for printers). By applying for a patent for the design a period of exclusivity is acquired. The profit made on the pads will be much higher than what is made on the machine itself. The machine can even be sold at a very low price in order to increase its market share, after which the sales of the pads will, of course, increase considerably. It is only once the patent expires that the competition starts, but by then the customers are already accustomed to a certain brand of pads. A clever manufacturer would have already introduced another revolutionary and improved type that requires a slightly different type of pad! Although the term 'prisoners strategy' has a negative ring to it, it doesn't have to be so. From the perspective of a business model the profit shifts from the core product to the supplies. And from the customer's perspective there is the advantage of a relatively cheap core product. The other costs are then spread out throughout the life of the product according to use.

Apple also employs this strategy, but has the additional advantage of being a trendsetter and market leader. In the 1990s the music industry came under a great deal of pressure through young people illegally copying CDs and the free downloading of music through websites such as Napster. The business model of the music industry began to feel the strain. What's more, people were still listening to music in a very traditional analogue manner. A physical music medium such as a CD (which replaced the LP) had to be bought in its entirety even if there were perhaps just one or two tracks on it that people wanted. Downloading made it possible to play the music in a different manner. But the memory capacity was still limited. With a Walkman this was due to the cassette and with the mp3-player this was on account of the memory. In 2001 Apple came up with a totally new concept. Initially it had a rather critical reception, but later people recognised that it could be a solution to the illegal downloading and playing of music. Apple's new mp3-player was highly sought-after thanks to its design, screen and large memory, but also simply because it was an Apple brand. The iTunes program was used to transfer the music onto the iPod. The music was made available in the Apple store. It was possible for customers to download an entire CD, but they could also buy just a single track. Apple paid royalties for the music, but the music industry did have to get used to the fact that people could buy per individual music track. In the past model, a popular song on the CD would be used to get buyers to purchase an entire CD. The iPod provided not only buyers but also an infrastructure; iTunes became the online music shop. As this was a prisoner situation, Apple made a great deal of profit with iTunes. For the iPhone a similar sort of buzz was created in 2007, and initially here, too, there was a prisoner situation. iPhone users were introduced to apps[3] that when touched could make a phone call or access a website (the first successful smartphone). The change was thanks to the apps on the iPhone and the multi-touch screen. The prisoner situation was primarily the contract with a telecom operator AT&T and the product's own operating system iOS. Due to the success of the iPhone, the smartphone became increasingly popular and users accustomed to a multi-touch screen with apps. Other suppliers were keen to replicate this functionality. In 2010 Apple introduced a new type of computer, the iPad, which also uses the multi-touch screen functionality and apps. What's more, the brand's own operating system, which was closed off to other suppliers, was used. As a result, iPad users had to download the apps from the Apple website. This was also a prisoner situation. The apps suppliers had to meet the required functionality for Apple, which led to a closed environment for only the owners of the Apple iPad only. In some cases the owner of the iPad had to pay for the app, but in many other cases it was the supplier. This has led to a great deal of irritation among other suppliers as Apple took this too far. One such example were the apps of newspapers and magazines whereby Apple also asked for 30% of the revenue of the subscription arranged via the app. As a result of the increasing criticism of this dependence and prisoner approach, Apple has become a little more flexible. What makes the Apple brand really stand out, however, is the revolutionary design of the Apple products. Apple seemed to be in a position to change the behaviour of the user as it did with the introduction of the multi-touch screen and apps. Due to this powerful market position, Apple is seen as a technological trendsetter. The new business model is certainly successful and the prisoner situation is not (yet) seen as a restrictive factor in the success of Apple and the enthusiasm of its uses.

---

3   App is an abbreviation of application, a program that is loaded onto the smartphone or tablet. Via this program a connection is made with a particular program on the Internet with information or a video.

SHORT TAIL, LONG TAIL

The solution for the existing retail might be the short tail/long tail principle. Sell only the short-tail articles in the shop, articles with a high emotional value for impulse buying and a high turnover rate. This way the investment in stocks will drop dramatically and customer will be surprised by the articles with a high hype value, being in fashion and in demand. These articles can be taken home directly. Articles with a lower turnover rate or articles that should be home delivered are long-tail articles. Sold through the webshop or terminals in the shop. A combination of 'click and collect' is possible or a combination with dropshipping. In this case the customers buy from the shop, no investment is needed for the shopkeeper and the Internet is integrated in the business model. This way shops can be much smaller, will be more surprising and a lower investment is needed. Using the existing technology with mobiles, terminals and tracking and tracing in a new business model will make retailing more attractive for customers, retailers and manufacturers. This kind of new business model is more future-proof than adapting the old models or reducing costs.

Conclusion and Summary of Chapter 6

Because market circumstances have changed and will continue to do so, retailers will have to see which business model is the most appropriate. An answer will have to be found to these changes, as well as to the strength of other parties and suppliers and to the customers' decision-making process. The traditional, transaction-oriented business model is not suitable for the future and this is what lies at the heart of the problems faced by retailers.

Table 6.1   Conclusion and summary

Business model	Characteristics	Role of the Internet
Traditional transaction model.	Profit on sales.	The same model.
Collaboration strategy.	Profit on transactions and collaboration, profit sharing.	Supplementary, the same model is also possible.
Multi-channel strategy.	Separate channels with separate strategy and pricing.	Separate channel with own strategy.
Customer-oriented strategy.	Profit per customer, *share of wallet*, often also profit on service products.	Part of the entire strategy. Often for communication and *near-field-communication*.

Table 6.1　　Continued

Business model	Characteristics	Role of the Internet
Modular strategy.	Competing main product, expensive dependent modules. Customer makes menu. Profit with modules.	Often for operating excellence of the core product.
Affiliate strategy.	Profit on affiliates, sometimes amount per lead, profit sharing also possible.	Part of the total affiliate strategy. Often also a strong strategy for integrating the Internet within the concept.
Cross-retailing strategy.	Customer-based. Unequivocal picture of the customer giving better control and service provision. Profit per customer.	Support of the entire buying process dependent on the behaviour of customers.
Captive/prisoner strategy.	Profit on captive customer, often extra supplies and components.	Support of the ordering process.

7

The End of Shops? A Fable or Reality?[1]

New developments are often placed within old frameworks. Retailers look to see which changes are possible and which problems they will solve. This is frequently done on a large scale, without really examining the motives of the individual.

Changes without Really Changing

The invention of the internal combustion engine led to a horse and carriage without the horse, but with still a driver at the 'reins'. The far cleaner streets were considered to be the greatest advantage of the car thanks to the dramatic reduction of horse droppings. This fact alone was enough for the car to be welcomed with open arms. People, however, quickly realised that this new form of transport also came with some drawbacks. A great deal of dust was whipped up, and the speed of the car posed an unexpected safety hazard. The infrastructure therefore had to be modified. Roads were paved (in order to prevent dust), pavements were laid to avoid accidents and later traffic lights were introduced to control the traffic. The problems that were solved in turn led to further problems that required new solutions. This did not involve any real fundamental changes. There was as yet no need for motorways or roundabouts, which would much later provide the answer to the further increasing traffic intensity.

And what about the discussions concerning the use of the mobile phone: who is really going to bother sending text messages? A phone, after all, is for talking! The mobile phone was simply an individualisation of telephone usage;

---

1   Various branch organisations are also studying the future retail landscape. An example of this is CBW-Mitex with the report *Retail 2020*, November 2010.

individuals now had their own telephone which was no longer confined to the house or a particular location. It was not really considered an innovation. It was only once the telephone became mobile that a new application arose. This was in the form of text messages, later apps and then the Internet.

With trains we still do not see any real innovations. Since their invention, the infrastructure has not changed at all. Even the standard railway gauge that was introduced by the Romans is still in use today. Any change to this would require an upheaval of the entire infrastructure. Only in Montreal do the underground trains uniquely run on rubber tyres for noise pollution reasons.

These days there are similar discussions regarding innovations. The gramophone record was first replaced by vinyl records, then by the CD. The first MP3 player was restricted to a fixed play order. It was only when downloading became all the rage that music tracks could be played in a preferred order. Book publishers, on the other hand, still have not found a suitable answer to the new reading behaviour. The answer is certainly not the e-book (after all, what's new?), but is more likely to be a combination of reading, videos and the Internet. Reading is more than just words and books. It involves stimulating the mind with knowledge or entertainment, with insight or recreation. In order to implement any innovation it is necessary to go back to the basics, because perhaps this objective can be achieved in a completely different way from producing a book. This also applies to the retail sector: back to the essence, the smallest unit, the customer. Simply adding Internet to the shop, or adding a certain experience by changing the set-up or by installing a video screen is not enough. This would just be a variation of the old theme of stimulating sales transactions. Retailers have to closely examine what lies at the heart of what they do. They have to look at the needs and wishes of the customer, the reasons why customers actually come to the shop and the way in which they want to pay for the services. This change will determine what sort of future awaits the retail sector. Retail in the future will nearly always be a combination of rational considerations and emotion, of physical and virtual, of transactions and loyalty/ bonding. The shop will feature various forms of Internet applications (plateau, terminal, mirror, mobile phone, checkout), but the shop itself will also be on the Internet with information, perhaps to sell, through affiliates and for buying support. It will be a mix of these factors and may vary according to the shop, sector and perhaps the target group as well. The biggest change, however, is that the focus will no longer be on products and selling, but on buying and customers.

Background to the Change

For many years the direct channel was not taken seriously. Mail-order companies, coupon deals, door-to-door salesmen were all marginal. In the 1980s, however, the world of direct marketing did make a splash but mainly in the area of communication. The new entrants to the retail market sporadically also led to reactions. Of course, IKEA had a large impact on home furnishing shops in the region, but the growth in the number of IKEA shops was rather slow. Shopping centres did emerge, but often no thanks to the protests of the retailers. In the meantime, shopping streets and shopping centres were taken over by large national players. And eventually every shopping street in the country seemed to look the same with seemingly identical shops, boring and uniform. Customers did complain, but nothing changed. However, often real pain has to be felt before something is finally done. Certain government policies contributed to the pain, such as pedestrianising shopping streets, taxing shops for using pavements and enforcing a rigid policy regarding opening hours. This all combined to put people off shopping. But then customers were given a choice. They were no longer prisoners of the retailers, the monotonous, uniform shopping streets or the rigid opening hours. Within a decade the power had shifted towards the customer, assisted by various technological developments such as the mobile phone, smartphone and the Internet. The various social developments also contributed to this shift in power; the increased mobility, rejuvenescence, more disposable income and a greater distance between home and work. As a result, people became increasingly willing to shop further away from home.

The major breakthrough of Internet came in 2008 and consequently the final blow for classical retailing. Of course the financial crisis (recession) in 2008 and the years to follow made customers and retailer realise that costs could be saved by using Internet. Customers embraced the transparency of the Internet, suddenly discovered lower prices (or the high margins of the retailers?) and understood that going to the shops was actually a choice, not a necessity. The increased leisure time, the wish to have quality time and the desire to be inspired and enjoy experiences in the physical world as well became stronger in response to the rationality of the technology. The products offered in the shops, however, were not geared up to this. Retailers employed old business models and did not often update the products. What's more, the monotonous shopping streets and boarded-up shop windows were not exactly inviting for customers wanting to have a fun day out. Furthermore, the shop staff and owners were not particularly welcoming when customers did come into the shops. You still sometimes have to force a smile from them! The financial crisis was a reason to reduce staff and staffing costs. Good. Experienced staff were replaced by cheaper staff with less knowledge. An extra stimulus for customers not to buy in shops anymore.

But 2008 was also the year of the breakthrough of the smartphone (introduced in November 2007) and later on the tablet (early 2010). Internet was no longer restricted to a computer especially when households used Wi-Fi, important for laptop computers. No longer was the customer restricted to a computer fixed with a cable to and Internet connection, but the use of Internet was wireless. Nowadays shopping is done on the couch in the evening. Partners are both online with laptop and iPad and are active on social media but also on webshops. The buying resistance in the evening, quite often after a few glasses of wine, is less than the next morning in the high street in the rain. Shopping on Internet became easy, fun and even social on the couch, especially after 10 o'clock.

> *Night-time shopping is growing over all. ChannelAdvisor, which runs e-commerce for hundreds of sites, says its order volumes peak about 8 p.m., and that shoppers are placing orders later and later: in 2011, the number of orders placed from 9 to midnight increased compared with previous years.*

> *A recent array of night-time offers sent to a shopper's email inbox included: from 6 to 9 p.m., a limited-quantity sale on fashions at Neiman Marcus; at 7.38 p.m., a promotion for three-day stays at Loews hotels; at 8.44 p.m., a promotion by Gilt for macaroons and faux-fur blankets; and at 2.23 a.m., an offer by Saks for a $2,000 gift card with purchase.*

Source: Stephanie Clifford, NYtimes.com, 27 December 2011.

If you walk down a shopping street in the evening after closing time, it can be quite alarming. And that image sometimes stays with you even to the next day! But suddenly retailers started to feel the pain; they realised that something had to be done. But what? The old pattern of the engine and the carriage was coming back. Shops now stay open longer. They have to provide an experience, but don't (and that smile still has to be pried from them). Retailers are looking to the Internet, but don't understand the new rules. They are all trying to get on top of the Google search list, tenaciously holding onto their company name as domain name, and regard quick deliveries as excessively demanding and too much bother.

They certainly don't have time for social media or Twitter. They still think that a website is all they need for driving the sales providing, of course, the website doesn't cost too much. After all, that money has to come out of their profits, their own pockets. Retailers have to realise, however, that there is now a new buying behaviour that cannot be reversed, and that the old (transaction-based) business model of the retail sector will no longer play a significant role. Future scenarios that are still based on optimising the current supply model will discover that there are new developments that had not been predicted. Customers make unexpected decisions, and essential human values such as communication, conviviality, security, trust and convenience will remain very important, also in the future.

The Traditional Retail Model

The traditional retail model is based on traders and buyers, on craftsmen and tailor-made work, on knowing and trusting one another. This model is based on the supply paradigm, where the product that is offered forms the leitmotif. The traditional marketing rules fit in well with this paradigm, as do the supplier's position of power, the frequently fixed prices based on cost price and market conditions and the strong focus on transactions … in other words: selling! Any innovations in the retail sector were always introduced within this concept. A fixed place of business instead of a mobile operation, grouping shops in shopping areas and shopping centres in order to encourage customers to visit, and improved deliveries from the manufacturer through automated ordering procedures. This made representatives who would visit the shops to take orders superfluous. The organisation of automation was also based on this supply driven model, with its focus on back-office automation and process automation. It is easy to place all the contemporary developments within this supply driven paradigm, the same retail landscape. The changes that have arisen due to the new buying behaviour have led to the Internet becoming important for information and buying. We now suddenly hear about a multi-channel approach, in other words doing the same thing in two channels. That is to say, repeating all activities involving the Internet. Everyone is throwing themselves onto the Internet as a new information, communication and purchasing channel; retailers, manufacturers and even consumers are offering their goods on the Internet. This is a change, of course, but is it not really just a variant of the old pattern of sales, of trying to bring about a transaction? The traditional retail model has not changed as a result of it. Something much more fundamental is going on in the retail sector; the older model is being attacked from all sides, by new entrants, the Internet, customers and their new behaviour and by suppliers. The old model cannot hold out to this. A new one will have to emerge that can respond to both the current possibilities and the buying motives of customers, the very basis of retail. The sales paradigm is changing into a demand paradigm. Not a product focus, therefore, but rather a focus on the needs and wishes of the customer.

In Retrospect

THE NEW BUYING BEHAVIOUR (THE NEW SHOPPING)

Breakdown of the Buying Process

Shops used to be the place where you would look around, search for information and buy. These days people tend to first look on the Internet at home. While sitting comfortably on their sofa, customers decide then and there what they are going to buy and where. Buying on the Internet is easy, but a physical shop is also an alternative as long as the customer can see benefits in going there. Top-of-mind is important, as customers have to be thinking about the shop. At the very least shops should have a website where visitors can find general information on the product range, the brands that are sold, the contact details and opening hours. The company would not even have to sell online, as long as the customer can see what is available, when and where. Competing with Internet suppliers is difficult. These webshops specialise in selling on the Internet just like the physical shops specialise in the buying moment, the personal contact.

The Internet: Friend or Foe

A website, with at the very least information about the shop itself, is an option. Direct communication with customers is possible through newsletters, email and microblogging (Twitter). This can help to strengthen the relationship with the customer. But the Internet in the shop is also a good alternative like The House of Fraser in Aberdeen. This allows customers to look at the product range online while in the shop, discuss the options with the salesperson and then buy straightaway. Sometimes they'll be able to take the product home with them immediately, sometimes it is delivered to their house. This enables the retailer to offer customers a far wider product range. The customer can consult with the salesperson, and the shop is able to put more emphasis on the social contacts. In the future, we shall see the Internet in the shop playing an increasingly important and integral role within the shop concept, with videos, smartphones and tablets. It is this integration of the physical aspect and the Internet that will make the shop a strong competitor again when it comes to selling products that require advice. This does not involve a multi-channel strategy but a cross-channel strategy

The Impact of Mobility and Mobile Services

Mobility and mobile services allow people to buy wherever they want. This may be at home (provisions), on the road or in a shopping centre. A car enables customers to buy from almost anywhere; the range has increased and the motives for buying can vary considerably. What's more, tablets, smartphones and targeted mobile communication have had a major impact. The ease of surfing and recognition that so typifies the Internet is also expected in the real world. 'Auto-id' systems whereby personal identification is possible, through the smartphone and the chip, and the cloud will become widely accepted. This will not only allow shops to send highly personal messages, but will also enable a personal *narrowcasting*, such as the *smart mirror* and the personal reflections in shop windows. This is a start of a personal experience and service within the retail sector.

THE COMPETITION /PRODUCT RANGE

The Impact of Moment-driven Product Range and Purchasing

Primark, MediaMarkt, 99p stores and the flash shops or pop-up stores are well geared up to the buying moment: perception, discounts and special offers. The feeling that this is your chance leads to a different type of buying behaviour. Retailers will increasingly support these impulse moments. It can be an impulse, but it can also be the last link in a buying process. The customer comes into the shop fully informed. The retailer therefore has to respond to this straightaway with targeted communication, good advice and an offer the customer cannot refuse. It is impulsiveness that will become even more important for retailers rather than calculated purchasing as carried out on the Internet. Once customers walk into the shop, they have to immediately be motivated to buy there through the friendly staff, hospitality, sound advice, the possibility of seeing the products and perhaps also by looking on the Internet for what they need together with the salesperson. A partnership has to emerge again whereby the salesperson does not focus on selling but rather helps the customer to buy. Retailers have to take advantage of the moment, by surprising, motivating and bonding with the customer.

The Impact of New Entrants

New entrants change the market circumstances. These days a website is often set up first and, if successful, a shop is then opened. These shops can have a support function for the products offered on the Internet, but are also intended to take advantage of the opportunities in the market. Due to far greater economies of scale, international chains are able to offer very affordable prices, and through these companies' own domestic market (Chinese shops) they are able to offer a different type of product range as well as much lower prices. The local shops simply cannot compete with this. Customers who shop on the Internet just as easily as in the physical shops are not particularly loyal. Every new entrant is a threat for physical shops. Just take a look at the success, or the threat, of Chinese shops, WallMart or Primark.

JOHN LEWIS STARTS ITS INTERNATIONAL EXPANSION IN THE NETHERLANDS

The British chain of department stores John Lewis opened a partly Dutch language webshop on Tuesday. Dutch consumers can visit the webshop for clothing and domestic goods, reports the Dutch newspaper De Financiële Telegraaf.

For John Lewis the website is the first step in its international expansion. 'If we are successful in our neighbouring countries, we will accept payment in euros and develop webshops that are targeted at specific countries,' says online manager Emma McLaughlin. Dutch consumers already know where to find the webshop of the British chain. Some 30,000 visitors of the website come from the Netherlands, explains McLaughlin. She is confident of success: 'In the first two hours we already had two sales from the Netherlands, and that without any marketing activities.'

Recently, the British chain of department stores Marks & Spencer, with Dutchman Marc Bolland at the helm, announced that they were again to open shops in West Europe.

Source: De Financiële Telegraaf, 22 June 2011.

The Impact of Large Out-of-town Centres

Customers are more than willing to visit the large out-of-town centres, often as part of a day out. The shopping is combined with other activities or fun for the children and is then often of secondary importance. The main objective is a fun day out; shopping is just part of it. These centres contribute to the creation of a new retail landscape, with plenty of parking facilities and special attractions such as restaurants, events and cinemas. This in turn helps to create space in the city centres for not only specialty shops, boutiques and fun shops, but also restaurants, cafes such as Starbucks, and bars. There will also be more space for leisure activities, such as cinemas, amusement arcades, discos, etc. In addition, smaller shops will emerge again in villages and residential areas. These will often be branches of large chain stores that offer a limited product range in the shop but have an associated webshop where everything is available. These online purchases can then be collected from the shop or even changed there if the customer so decides. Extra traffic is created because the customer comes into the shop not only to buy something, but also to collect or change the ordered article. The shop function will change as a result, but as part of a total shop concept this will be profitable. It is up to town centres to change and see in new role in fun shopping, in recreation with culture, nightlife and restaurants. But even people will move back to town centres because they are single or older people because of the culture and fun. Shops will adapt with a mixture of shops for day-to-day shopping like small grocers and small household shops but also with luxury shops like small boutiques and lifestyle shops. But was this also not the case in olden days?

The Impact of New Concepts

New concepts, such as the above-mentioned *click and collect*, are interesting for the current physical retail sector. But also other concepts whereby the retailer becomes a service point for suppliers. The stocks remain the property of the manufacturer, and payment is only settled once the articles are sold, either in the shop or on the Internet. Other possibilities involve a website that can be directly linked to a manufacturer, the so-called *embedded* solution. Here use is made of the familiarity and trust of a local shop, but the sales go through the manufacturer or importer. Here too, products can be changed at the shop. The margins on all the sales are for the retailer, because it is he who has the contact and relationship with the customers. It is these sorts of new concepts that are interesting for the retailer as they result in a lower financial need, the partnership with the suppliers becomes the basis for the shop concept and the retailer can take on the traditional function again: to be there for the customer. New concepts such as the modular concept, affiliate concept and *subscriptions* are also based on individual customer wishes and lead to a greater bond with the retail sector. Creativity is required in order to find the right concept for the customer, the target group and the branch. A new development is the concept stores where you can buy everything for a certain topic, the adventure stores or a shop like 'birthday'. Also in other shops concepts are more important, customers no longer have to search departments to find everything for let say holiday, Easter, weddings or a birthday. All relevant articles are combined in a certain place with the right look and feel and sometimes even music (musical spotlights).

Other shops go for fun like Hamleys, a kid's paradise.

SUPPLIERS AND COLLEAGUES

Collaboration and Affiliates

Collaboration in particular is important to the retail sector. This will be necessary to attract customers, which can be done in, for example, shopping centres. But it can also be done by referring to one another, the affiliate principle whereby specialty shops support one another through *cross-referrals*. For example, if you buy a suit you may get a discount coupon for a pair of shoes from the neighbouring shoe shop, or a coupon for a free cup of coffee and cake around the corner. Such referrals with a discount, loyalty points and the like can stimulate the customer to buy more in the shopping centre. It is also possible to jointly manage a website that provides information on the shopping centre and perhaps also features a joint buying concept, whereby the attention of potential customers is drawn to the products of the various shops (*associate selling*). This is the same as with webshops that provide information, such as 'other customers also bought these items' or a referral to suitable accessories. These items may also be products sold by fellow retailers.

Other possibilities for collaboration are, for example, jointly developing an app with information for customers, developing a mobile concept for *location-based services*, and carrying out special offers and joint communication. It is by collaborating that a centre can become much more attractive to customers and costs can be shared. Customers in turn can benefit from the smaller-scale shops but still enjoy the benefit of the shopping centre's total concept. Here in particular the Internet and mobile network play an important role. Through direct communication via the Internet or the mobile telephone, attention can be drawn to other products (association) or referrals made to fellow retailers (affiliates). Collaboration can, of course, also take place on the Internet by providing a joint selling platform, managing a website together or jointly producing a newsletter.

Focus of the Retailer

The web retailer has a strong focus on the customer. Thanks to the technology, he knows his customer, knows how long the customer has been on the website and what he has looked at. The web retailer can respond to this by making new special offers based on the customer's behaviour on his site. This strong customer focus is the strength of the Internet. Retailers have traditionally been focused not so much on customers but on the product, location and selling. In order to successfully respond to the threats of the Internet, it is also essential to focus on customers. The retailer has to know the customers, communicate directly with them and set up a customer database. Newsletters can be sent as well as personalised special offers. A loyalty concept can also form part of this. This concept is much more than just a discount card or a stamp card, but will lead to true loyalty based on knowledge, surprises and advice. It is the automatic identification that is possible these days with (chip) cards such as London's Oyster travel card and with the smartphone that enables a new form of loyalty. Retailers will have to increase their customer orientation if they are to remain successful.

NEW WEAPONS

New Business Models

It can be quite a challenge for businesses to rethink their business model. What do customers want to pay for and what is the best way for customers to determine the final amount due? Ryanair, Apple and telecom providers have all succeeded in using new models. Key to their successes was looking at where there would be benefits for the customer: in the modules (Ryanair), in the services (apps), or in the fixed price (telecom companies). In the past, customers came to the shop in order to buy a particular article. There wasn't a great deal of choice, so the actual presence of the articles provided some value to the customer. But now that you can buy them everywhere and anytime, people carefully look at the price. What are the shop's benefits and what is its value? Focusing on the look and feel, experience or image is fine, but can easily be copied. So is this the solution for shops? Customer bonding is better when done in a way that customers truly want and appreciate it.

Now that it can no longer be taken for granted that customers will buy in a shop, the logic of a transaction-based business model has disappeared. Retailers have to be more creative, think anew about the proposition and, in particular, not do this alone. Entering into a partnership with the secondary suppliers can form a good foundation; a relationship based on a win-win principle. Retailers have to re-establish the value and benefits for the customer and then determine how to share the profits. A model such as the one Miele now employs for its Internet sales is an example of this. Also the decision of the Dutch mail-order company Wehkamp to act as fulfilment provider for C&A among others is a good variant. A partnership with secondary suppliers, with customers and with colleagues. Although the world seems to be becoming increasingly harder and more individual, partnership and bonding will be the enduring models for the future. Social media are perhaps the best examples of this.

Customers

Customers will determine the future for the retail sector. The buying motives of individual customers will dictate what is bought and where. These buying motives can vary according to product, target group and even gender. Men have a greater interest in and affinity with technology, electronics and cars, whereas women are generally more interested in clothing, shoes and children's clothes. Gender in itself is not important; it is important, however, that retailers appeal to the right target group. The right message, the right purchase support at the right time and also with the right proposition. A few years ago, Sainsbury's in England introduced a baby concept whereby young parents paid a fixed amount per week for baby food during the first two years of their child. The preference and the age of the child was recorded in the database. Each week a baby food package was set aside for the young parents. This subscription concept, for a service provided by the shop for a fixed amount per week, is a good example of a loyalty concept.

Internet

The Internet is a threat for the traditional retail sector. The threat is twofold. Thanks to the Internet, the customer is better informed than he used to be; all the information is available on many websites and users give one another tips through social networks. This knowledge often exceeds that of the salesperson. The recession has also led to frequent reductions in the training and quality of sales staff, which further exacerbates this disparity in knowledge. Customers are beginning to see no real added value to visiting shops (they think: I know more about it than the sales staff anyway) and are increasingly inclined to buy on the Internet. And this is the second threat for the traditional retail sector. Buying on the Internet is easy, convenient and these days also reliable thanks to, for example, the home shopping quality mark and the possibility to change articles as well. As a result, local retailers have to suddenly compete with webshops that can be set up anywhere. This threat is growing considerably. Internet use among the age group 10 and older will soon reach the 100% mark.

> *'It's the same consumers who are buying computers in one department as are buying curtains in another,' he says. 'So increasingly we need to offer personalised services to people who need to get kit set up.' The Apple Store's own one-to-one service offers a similar idea.*

When it comes to personal service, however, customers are increasingly set to see companies using their Facebook or Twitter profiles to get in touch. Marc Benioff is the CEO of Salesforce.com, the web-based software that powers thousands of businesses. At the company's conference in London this week, Mr Benioff showed how companies are increasingly monitoring what is said about them online.

That focus on service, whether it's personalised via social media and about selling cars, computers or watches, is where many retailers see their future. As John Lewis's Matt Leeser observes, 'It's the environment and the staff.'

Source: Matt Warman, *Daily Telegraph*, 9 April 2012.

But there will also be opportunities for retailers in the future. Collaboration with, for example, suppliers and a mention of the local sales outlets on the suppliers' websites can lead to greater online visibility. The Internet in the shop will also provide opportunities, with video terminals next to products and, in particular, mobile Internet. Direct communication at the place of purchase is a strong weapon. In addition, direct communication provides new suppliers such as Groupon and Social Living the possibility of attracting new customers. The Internet is therefore certainly a major threat, but a smart retailer can turn this threat into an effective weapon in his battle for the customer. The last thing any retailer should do is to wait, refuse to change and complain. Then they really will drive the customer away to the Internet.

Conclusion and Summary of Chapter 7

Table 7.1   Conclusion and summary

Focus point	Threat	Modification
Internet	Webshops, transparency, low prices, direct communication, customer knowledge, customer focus.	Focus on customers, direct communication by Internet but also on-site.
Suppliers	Own sales via flagstores and the Internet. Lower margins through increased marketing efforts.	Collaboration, functional division, partnership, clear agreements regarding earnings model.
Customers	Less loyalty, buying on the Internet, negotiating price, well-informed.	Pamper, surprise, direct communication, be proactive, offer convenience, service orientation, take customers' needs as a basis.

Table 7.1   Continued

Focus point	Threat	Modification
New customer behaviour.	Shopping is recreation, orientation and looking for information on the Internet, breakdown of the buying process. Strength of social media and mobile Internet. Wanting to be individual, but still wanting to bond.	Develop loyalty, relationship-based instead of transaction-based. Integration of technology (Internet and shop), mobile, video, personal contacts and advice.
Competition.	Quicker, more active, better promotions, more creative, better customer contact, better direct communication. Sophisticated Internet strategy.	Different, better, innovative but in particular service oriented, appealing service and product range, listen and communicate well. Communication is the weapon against the competition.
Location.	Empty premises, the wrong product range, no parking or shabby appearance. Not modern, nor attractive to customers.	Dare to change location. Look for a magnet or like-minded parties, make location attractive and accessible. New models such as *click and collect* provide space for smaller shops.

Research on Retailing and Web Retailing

Revolutionary Road, New Shopping Streets[1]

There is a small revolution going on in retail in England that will have major consequences for city centres and nearby properties. A popular shopping street is part of an infrastructure with shops and houses that are within walking distance from which they also derive a certain value. According to a study carried out in England the value of property is 12% higher if it is close to a shopping centre.

Currently we can see a major change in shopping streets. We see cheap shops moving into areas and setting up alongside more expensive ones, and that is not good for property prices. This is a fundamental change. The ease and convenience of out-of-town shopping centres and the Internet is changing the way the shopping streets are being used. If a shopping street wants to survive this change, it will have to change with it. According to architect Sir Terry Farrel this means that shops are becoming more of a showroom as customers e-shop and want to see, feel and compare. Due to the new type of shops and the customers' different motivation, the shopping street will also become increasingly varied. The centre or the shopping street will become a place with all forms of cultural, social and economic activities that make use of the new technology and improved connectivity.

This will lead to a wider and, from a customer's point of view, a more practical range of services being offered, whilst there will still be shops selling provisions and clothes. Earls Court High Street will generally be less shop orientated, and will have a greater focus on training courses, culture and art. A computer shop will therefore be close to IT training institutes, and solicitors'

---

1   Revolutionary Road, *Financial Times*, 2 July 2011, p. 4: House & Home, summary.

offices next to an art gallery, a cafe and perhaps also a beauty parlour. Festivals, street fairs and other activities are necessary in order to remain successful and attractive. Earls Court High Street was inspired by Marylebone High Street, a model of an innovative, independent and successfully varied, community-oriented street.

'We wanted to attract tenants who had just that little bit more to offer than tenants of an average shopping street', says Toby Shannon, CEO of Howard de Walden Estate, which manages 70% of the shop properties in this street. In addition to restaurants, cafes and fashion shops, there are art galleries on Marylebone High Street and each year a summer fair is organised. The great variety and the quality of the shops has a significant impact on the local commercial real estate and house prices.

Despite the success of these streets and the impact on the value of property, they remain exceptions. It is very difficult to get owners of real estate and retailers to work together. It is a challenge for the local authorities to collaborate with businesses, retailers included, and house owners in order to change the shopping streets and shopping centres and to be creative with the empty premises. But if successful, this will be a wonderful improvement for customers. The 'High Street' will become much more pleasant and interesting as well as more community-oriented than it is today.

In-Store Shopping versus eShopping

Examining the Internet in terms of consumer marketing and more specifically consumer behaviour is more than necessary at this time when the Internet is integrated into our day-to-day lives. Understanding the way consumers make decisions for a shopping mode will provide important theoretical contributions to the marketing world. Based on this knowledge more effective and meaningful strategies can be formed. Research suggests that when visiting a physical store can be made with little effort, in-store shopping is preferred over e-shopping. This is quite remarkable since online stores are know for being convenient and offer better product selections to consumers. Consumers explore the product in a physical store but could then decide to buy the product online because the consumer can purchase the product cheaper in an online store. This shows that price will still remain a major factor in consumer store choice. Obviously, the choice between online and offline shopping lies not only in time and cost. Sociodemographic and personality characteristics factors also play a role.

Younger people under the age of 25, males, highly educated and consumers from higher income groups are more likely to partake in Internet shopping. Also, consumers who often engage in online shopping and have positive online shopping experiences are more likely to repeat this activity.

Looking at personality characteristics, a high self-efficacy will lead to consumers that perceive themselves as capable to engage in e-shopping. As mentioned in the critical success factors, a way online retailers could make shopping more comfortable is facilitating the ease of use of their storefront. This will also mean that consumers do not have a high degree of expertise. Another characteristic that plays a role in the mode of shopping is the need for interaction. Consumers with a high need for interaction will be more likely to prefer in-store shopping. Online retailers could lower this barrier by being more responsive and interactive. This will also heighten the perceived service quality which is one of the critical success factors for online shops. Product characteristics that are standardised, digital and have a high degree of familiarity are more successful in online retailing. However, this does not dictate that there is a set rule of products that can be successfully sold on the Internet. Finally, with regards to personality characteristics, a lack of trust is one of the most important factors that prevent consumers from choosing e-shopping over in-store shopping. The degree of trust can be influenced by dealing with the perceived privacy and safety issues.

Naturally, online and psychical stores both have their advantages and disadvantages. It is up to the consumers to make a trade off between the advantages and disadvantage in order to make a choice in the shopping mode. This depends on the different factors that were discussed previously, but also on the shopping process. In the shopping process the most important components that were most influenced by the emergence of the Internet were: information gathering, transaction/purchase and delivery. The search of information on the Internet is far more superior than to psychical stores. Where the evaluation part was traditionally a separate component, nowadays the evaluation also takes place in the information search stage. Consumers find that consumer ratings and consumer reviews are the most important in finding information about a certain product/service. This means that consumers are influenced by the opinions of others at an early stage. Therefore it is important for online retailers to monitor the online reviews of their products. The retailers should also be active and offer incentives when consumers are dissatisfied. Another factor that plays a major role in the consumers' trade of in shopping mode is the delivery. The longer the waiting time, the less consumers want to buy from the Internet. For digital products waiting time is non-existent. Retailers are trying to bridge the time between purchase and delivery by offering discount coupons, personalised packaging, track and tracing. This does not really shorten the delivery time but in the mind of the consumer it does because transparency is created. Also, by offering a click-and-collect service, consumers can choose to pick the products up instead of waiting for delivery. The transaction security issue can prevent consumers from adopting online shopping. This perceived risk can be diminished by creating trust in consumers. The underlying assumption of the previous factors is those consumers have to make a choice between e-shopping and in-store shopping. However, this is not always necessary. E-shopping and in-store shopping can also be combined. Consumers can fully substitute one mode of shopping for the other, one mode can activate the other mode, e-shopping can change the characteristics of in-store, complementary and it is also possible that no relationship occurs.

Since e-shopping has gained momentum it has led to more consumer power. There is a lot of competition on the world wide web and only a few survive. The only way to survive is to offer superior service quality. The best way to establish this is by building strong relationships with consumers. This breads loyalty, which then leads to retention and therefore a successful e-commerce shop.

Conclusion of research carried out by Naoual el hachioui and Sabrina Mekaiel, RSM/ErasmusUniversity, Rotterdam.

How to Integrate Technology into Buying

Let's start with *QR-codes*. QR-codes allow companies to place a scannable barcode on an advertisement which links consumers to their website. But then again, the problems arise of selling furniture online. Almost all QR-codes are scanned with mobile devices, so they always have a small screen to view anything that the QR-code links them to. Place QR-codes in advertisements, but instead of linking it to their website, link it to a new technique. Google Maps is currently popular due to its Google Street view option, which enables the user to look at a panoramic photograph and scroll through the streets in every city or town. This new technique will make use of this knowledge, but then apply it to a store. The retailer will create panoramic photographs of their store and give the user the option to scroll through the store, to give that feeling of an in-shop-experience. The QR-code will link to this Shop View, which is then shown on the mobile device. It is just like a movie that goes through the furniture shop, but it is interactive. It can easily be viewed on a small screen and enables the customer to view the furniture in a certain setting, the sizes compared to other objects and what the store looks like. This way, QR-codes can reach a large market due to their mass advertisement, but still generate that extra feeling that is needed with furniture.

Track and Trace is hardly used by retailers. This is strange since Track and Trace is a method to keep a customer satisfied during the waiting for the product to be delivered. The customer can keep in touch on the whereabouts of their product and can see what is currently being done to it. Now, if you take furniture, furniture often has a long delivery time due to its customisability and no/low stock. Sofas often even take six to eight weeks to deliver. Track and Trace can mean a lot for furniture retailers. It can satisfy the customers while they wait the eight weeks for their sofa to be delivered. They can see exactly in what process their customised sofa currently is. This is extremely convenient for those long term delivery times, but it can also be used for smaller products.

Dropshipping is a model that is kind of already used as a business model for luxury goods and furniture retailers. Retailers often have no or little stock due to the size of the products and the flexibility needed of these products (different fabrics, different shapes or different colours). This makes inventory not efficient. So they often send an order to the manufacturer, which delivers it to the retailers, which in turn delivers it to the customer. This is like drop-shipping. But why don't retailers and manufacturers use the dropshipping model in a way that the manufacturer delivers it to the homes of the customers. This of course increases the logistics costs of the manufacturer, since they have to bring it all the way to the customer, but it has some advantages as well. For the manufacturer, it provides some brand-awareness and gives the option to adjust products in case of wrong deliveries or damages. The retailer does not need inventory and can focus on the customers: selling and services. They do not have to worry about big logistical deliveries and reputational damage that comes with wrong deliveries from the factory. Dropshipping also makes it possible to operate internationally. The retailer does not need stores outside the country, but sells through the Internet site, while the manufacturer delivers to the customer.

Virtual reality has become affordable for companies. Especially with furniture, the customers want the option to customise their sofas, tables and other furniture. The websites analysis showed that the websites are decent enough to enable virtual reality. Why not insert an option to customise a sofa by clicking different colours, making different shapes, adding different kind of seats or change the fabrics (the use of configurators). And after these are ready, the results can be printed and brought to the store or even enable an order button so that the retailer can order it at the manufacturer.

Last, *Google Analytics* is an excellent tool to enhance the retailer's online website usage, especially if they combine it with QR-codes and virtual reality. With Google Analytics, they can examine how many people visit their website through a QR-code, since they can see how much that page has been referred to and the browser/device used. Google Analytics can be used for their online marketing purposes and to see which product in their collection is one of the most popular and which is the least. This gives them an indication of which products are likely to be popular in their offline shop as well, so that they can get rid of the low-selling products from their store. This is important since furniture products are often displayed in a certain setting, these settings take up a couple of square meters in the shop. Getting rid of low-selling products can save those areas for products that are a lot more popular. This increases the revenue per square meter.

As for the websites, most websites are decent looking and user-friendly. But not a lot of retailers are getting the full potential out of their websites. Retailers need to consider their websites as the online version of your offline shop. Of course, selling furniture online will always remain a problem, but virtual reality can help achieve this in a way so products are viewed better, can be customised through all the possible options and show the different fabrics. The products will be viewed with an option to zoom until the fabric can be examined, show a dropdown list of all possible fabrics, but one the most important features really has to be virtual reality. Nowadays it's affordable and enables customers to play around with different settings and choose their product online. This will not only increase customer satisfaction, but their design will also bind them to the retailer's shop, since the design comes from this retailer and the customer knows that it can be ordered through this very retailer. This stops them from looking further and not knowing if their favourite design is also available elsewhere. Also, Track and Tracing needs to be integrated with the website of the retailer. It increases the patience of the customer and because it is on the website and it is convenient for the customer to reach. The language option might be interesting to implement for international retailers, or retailers who expect a lot of foreign customers.

Conclusion of research carried out by Tom Duivenvoorden, RSM/Erasmus Univeristy, Rotterdam.

How Will Shops Survive?

Have a website! Customers are searching the net at their ease at home. While searching they should also see local shops. Each local shop should, at least, have a website and email function. Show opening times, collections, routes to the shop, latest news and ask for email addresses for a newsletter. Customers might consider to going to the shop instead of buying at a webshop!

> *Nearly half of all UK consumers are using the web to find the best local shops, a new study has found. The 2011 American Express Spendsetters Report found that 46% of British consumers now shop locally and 32% said that they 'now mainly shop for everyday purchases from local sources'. A similar number (31%) said sourcing local products is 'a priority when making essential purchases'.*
>
> *The so-called 'New Villagers' support their local economy and, American Express suggests, the growth in their numbers has been driven by 'the exponential growth of business to consumer social networking'. The report found that 'shoppers are sharing information on local forums and Twitter to advise other members of The New Villager group on local shopping finds and tips'.*
>
> *Source:* Matt Warman, *Daily Telegraph*, 20 July 2011.

Local shops are important for a local community. More and more time is spent in one's home, working at home, more leisure time, single households and the elderly generation. Local shops are important and should focus on community-oriented retailing, offer products and services for the daily needs.

> *Aurora Fashions, the group behind leading fashion brands Coast, Oasis and Warehouse, is set to increase online sales across its brands by a third with the launch of Anywhere Everywhere, a new approach to stock management and order fulfilment that opens up the stock inventory across all sales channels, maximising satisfaction of customer demand.*
>
> *Opening up the inventory in this way means that orders for items which are sold out on the brand websites can be fulfilled from across the entire store portfolio, ensuring crucial sales are not lost. In a recent six week pilot of Anywhere Everywhere in selected stores, availability of products online increased by 28%, driving additional sales of over £2.5m. Online conversion rates doubled during the period of the pilot.*

The launch of Anywhere Everywhere represents a move by Aurora from multi-channel to omni-channel retailing, which aims to merge digital commerce with physical retailing to create a seamless experience for the customer. It represents a new model for stock management in retail, opening up stock inventory across the full store portfolio and replacing the traditional approach where stock has to be reserved for larger or online stores.

Mike Shearwood, Chief Executive of Aurora Fashions, commented: 'With Anywhere Everywhere, we're saying to customers "If we have it anywhere in the UK, we'll get it to you wherever you want it," which is a powerful message in today's climate. It gives every store the opportunity to boost sales by fulfilling web orders and enables even the smallest stores to have access to the brand's full product range, even much sought after limited edition pieces.'

Source: Aurora, December 2011.

Integrate click and collect. Have a small stock of articles for the normal needs but offer a wide range of articles on the Internet. Click and collect within 24 hours in the local shop. In combination with dropshipping the investment is much lower, the needed floor space is much less and the break-even level lower. This makes it easy to be profitable as a local shop.

Offer services *like home delivery* within an hour. This cannot be beaten by Internet, not only for food but especially for non-food. Within a certain range of the shop this service can be offered like is done by Aurora:

Aurora Fashions is launching 90 minute deliveries across all its brands in five new cities across the UK, becoming the first fashion retailer to do so.

The service, part of Aurora's strategy to offer its customers the widest range of delivery options on the market, allows customers to order and receive their fashion items within as little as 90 minutes by selecting this option at the checkout on the brands' websites. The service is being launched tomorrow in Birmingham, Liverpool, Bristol, Cardiff, Belfast and areas surrounding the Lakeside Shopping Centre in Thurrock.

Source: Aurora, 3 October 2011.

Communicate, webshops are very active in communication with newsletters, emailing and bannering. Shops do not even know the email address of their customers. Ask them, make a customer file and communicate by email! Even better, make a loyalty card to register the buying behaviour and communicate. Even go a step further by providing in-store offers for loyalty card holders. Use mobiles for in-store communication, direct and personal. But above all start with an email address and communicate. A relationship is built upon communication and this is one of the major mistakes of physical retailers. Customers do not come in the shop anymore so motivate and communicate directly through other sources.

Use technology, especially terminals and location-based services. When customers are in the shop motivate them to buy, help them to buy. Offer terminal support, Wi-Fi and if needed augmented reality support. Make use of the moment and the presence of customers. Before, one in ten visitors to a shop bought something; nowadays it is one in three (based upon Dutch research). In particular, Google is leading with new applications like Google view, iGoogle, Google shopping, Google circular and Google wallet. Google likes to support their users where ever they are, a good opportunity for retailers.

> *Google is testing a new kind of ad unit called 'Circulars', designed to mimic the full-page inserts traditionally found in newspapers. These large-format ads act like destination sites, where users can explore specials being promoted at nearby retail locations. The ad format is scheduled to be unveiled formally at an Advertising Week event in Manhattan later this week, a Google spokesperson tells* Mashable.

> *The ads, which will be personalized based on a number of factors including location and query, will pop up when viewers click on search or display ads. The ad format is compatible with desktop, mobile and tablet devices. In an interview with Bloomberg, Nick Fox, VP of product management at Google, said Circulars were designed in response to retailers' requests for advertising that would drive online visitors into offline stores.*

> *Source*: Laura Indvik, www.mashable.com, 3 October 2011.

In short, motivate people to visit the store and buy!

Conclusion:
Fundamental Changes Needed
for Retailing

From Supply-Driven to Internet-Based

In the old structure retailing was a supply-driven model based on a supply chain and a single distribution point, the retail shop. Manufacturers made articles to be sold in shops. In the various links in the supply chain the focus was on the next link – manufacturer, wholesaler, retailer and the final customer. Manufacturers call retailers their customers, but retailers talk about customers when they talk about the final customer. In this model a manufacturer and a retailer advertise, the retailer about the articles in the shop and the manufacturer about their brands. This model is one of dependency but not of harmony. They need each other but struggle about pricing and conditions.

The Classical Retail Model

The retailer likes a low price, a high margin and a delayed paying period. In some cases it is possible to sell the article in, say, 30 days but the manufacturer is paid in 90 days. The positive cash flow of the retailer can be invested in the shop, in stocks or in growth.

The manufacturer will stimulate the retailer to buy more articles by using in-store promotion, trade bonuses and advertising. The risk of non-sales is in most cases a risk for the retailer. The business model for a manufacturer is based on profit on sales and the aim is to sell as much as possible to the retailers (and indirectly to the end customer). Price, brand, channel strategy and product appearance are important elements for the manufacturer.

Retailers focus on store layout, location and shopping experience (including service and staffing).

As stated in this book, this model is losing its value because of the difference in shopping behaviour of customers, the use of Internet and maybe also the impact of recession. The classical retail model has changed because of:

- Multi-channel possibilities and different shopping preferences of customers.

- Out-of-town shopping centres with a very specific shopping experience. They are easy to reach, have good parking facilities, offer non-stop shopping, long opening hours and entertainment and food and drink facilities. Also, the shops are focused on social buying supported by restaurants, coffee shops and other pleasure driven suppliers – a different shopping experience than town shopping or Internet shopping.

- The new customer behaviour. For example, looking on the Internet, checking in the shop and buying where it suits best (e.g. Internet), will change the retail landscape. 'Show-rooming' is a major factor for the present retail. The new customer likes checking the Internet at home, looking at the products in the shop and buying on the Internet for a lower price, quite often with the mobile in the shop. For BestBuy, the biggest electronics retailer in the USA, this is a nightmare. People in the shop will buy direct with their mobile the same product on Amazon.com, which is always about 8% cheaper. Retailers have not found the right answer yet for this new behaviour and lowering the price also has a limit.

Frictions in the Classical Model

Diminishing sales for physical shops and increasing sales for webshops is a logical consequence and will lead to shop closures in every location. Predictions in Western Europe and the USA expect by 2020 that 25% of not-daily purchases will be done on the Internet. This is a big loss for the physical shops. Therefore, we need fewer shops, and shops in a different location to suit the customer better as described in this book. Convenience shopping, close at home and in locations where the customers are (like public transport stations) – shops for recreation and entertainment (fun shopping) and town centres for social shopping. The old model will not suit the new customer shopping behaviour which will lead to shop closures in the old shopping precincts, a price battle between shops and suppliers, financial risk with the shops and stocks, and finally, the costs of running the shops will be too high. The signs are so obvious when you walk through town centre shopping precincts or villages in England, France, Germany and the Netherlands.

A New Retail Model Needed

Based on this new customer behaviour and the impact on the classical retail model a fundamental change is needed. No longer is the basis a rigid supply-driven supply chain, but the buying moment. When do customers buy and when is stock needed? The split between the buying moment and delivery can also be implemented in traditional retailing. This change is based on a different offering for products with a high turnover rate and products with a low turnover rate. Articles with a high turnover rate are in demand and customers like to see and buy immediately; these articles should be sold in shops and shops should stock these articles. Articles with a low turnover rate

Table C.1   The new retail model

Articles in shop (short tail)	Articles to be sold differently (long tail)	Consequences for physical shops
Sold in shop and Internet.	Sold on Internet but also on terminals (apps) through Internet in shops.	Less stock needed in shops.
High turnover rate per article. Emotional products, impulse buying.	Low turnover rate per article Rational products	Terminals in shops, Wi-Fi, stock in warehouse or manufacturers.
More concept driven.	Unlimited supply with affiliates and arrangements with manufacturers.	More support en service for customers, concept stores based on a theme (holidays, birthdays) or subjects or objects (house, children).
Smaller shops on locations where the customers are.	Home delivery, same day delivery, next day delivery, click and collect.	Dropshipping arrangements. More communication with customers: newsletters, mailings, alerts, Apps. Direct, behaviour-based communication needed and in-store communication and location-based services (mobile).
More opportunities for small shops and individual shopkeepers.	New arrangements between suppliers and retailers. Cooperating and risk sharing. More cooperation with other retailers	More fun, more service, integrated with Internet, mobile and physical presence. Flexible renting/lease models based on turnover, traffic, location and floor space.

could be sold in the shop, but just as easily on the Internet. 'Same day' or 'next day' delivery is no objection for customers. By stocking mainly high turnover rated articles in the shops and low turnover articles on demand (via Internet) the new retail shops will be smaller, more attractive, and less capital will be needed. Therefore it is easier to open these kinds of shops and to open more shops in different locations. An example is the House of Fraser department store with terminal shops of 100 m², with direct access to Internet and home delivery or 'click and collect' in the shop.

Shops Should Facilitate Shoppers

This new retail model is based on the new way customers shop and on the expectations of the shoppers. Shopping is fun and customers should be motivated to go shopping. An omni-channel approach where the Internet is integrated in this new way of shopping is essential. Going to town should be fun with small boutique-like shops; these shops should surprise people. Towns need cheap parking facilities close to shops, restaurants and pubs. In towns, a nice shopping route should be possible, a kind of circle to walk to shops and plenty of stopping places for a bite, a drink, culture, or just a nice view. In particular, towns with a rich history have a big advantage in this regard. Small shops are more fun than big shops and owner-based shops can surprise shoppers more than chain stores can. And to top it, small shops are less expensive in lease costs, inventories and will have less stock.

The new model is based on a close relationship with suppliers, a risk-sharing model and more support from the supplier to the retailer. There is risk from inventories/stocks, long payment periods and maybe home delivery arranged by the supplier. A new model to fit this is dropshipping: customers buy through the shop, or the webshop, and the order is directly placed by a supplier. They will arrange delivery to the customers – no investment, no risk for the retailer, only the margin/bonus. The retailer will keep the ownership of the customer for communication and support. Dropshipping will make it possible to sell a wide range of articles to customers without extra investment and risks. More and more suppliers from the south of Europe are supporting webshops in Western Europe this way. The customer support and sales are done through the webshop of a local company. The order is placed directly by the supplier in, say, Spain. Delivery within 24 hours is guaranteed. Payment can go directly to a special bank account or through the retailers. Dropshipping can change retailing on a global way.

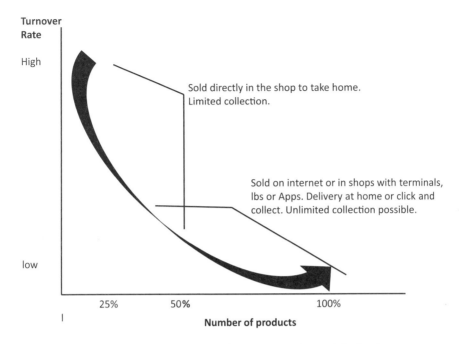

Figure C.1   New retail model based on integration with the internet

Solving the Mismatch between Supply and Customer Demand

Retailing is changing because the frictions in the buying process are too high for the retailer:

- Less turnover in shops; 25% of the non-food sales are Internet sales.

- Total transparency through Internet will lead to a battle on price.

- Different competitors with foreign Internet suppliers.

- High location costs for physical shops, high prices for floor space in shops, location costs and stock risks.

- New competition from out-of-town shopping centres, with no parking charges, long opening hours, modern shops and nice facilities for fun and recreation.

- And of course, the way of shopping (shopping 3.0) leads to show-rooming and price comparisons.

The future is bright when shopkeepers anticipate this new way of shopping and integrate Internet, mobiles and location-based services into their model.

- Shops should entertain and offer services, communicate directly and offer a personal service to their customers; they should also offer services through the website, through mobiles (apps), mobile alerts and the Internet via mailing, newsletters and banners.

- A retailer should focus on the needs of customers and focus on the relationship with customers.

- Financial risks, stock risks and Internet support are a partnership with suppliers and manufacturers. Only if they work together in a new short-tail/long-tail retail model will there be harmony in retailing. There should be a concentration of shops to suit the needs of the shopper and to add fun to the shopping process. The magnet of the shop is the loyalty of the shopper, the service of the shopkeeper and a total offering through partnerships. Only if retailing will make this happen will shoppers be loyal and retail shops have a future.

Mary Portas, Adviser of David Cameron (MP)

RECOMMENDATIONS FOR THE HIGH STREET (2011)

1. Put in place a 'Town Team': a visionary, strategic and strong operational management team for high streets.

2. Empower successful Business Improvement Districts to take on more responsibilities and powers and become 'Super-BIDs'.

3. Legislate to allow landlords to become high street investors by contributing to their Business Improvement District.

4. Establish a new 'National Market Day' where budding shopkeepers can try their hand at operating a low-cost retail business.

5. Make it easier for people to become market traders by removing unnecessary regulations so that anyone can trade on the high street unless there is a valid reason not to.

6.   Government should consider whether business rates can better support small businesses and independent retailers.

7.   Local authorities should use their new discretionary powers to give business rate concessions to new local businesses.

8.   Make business rates work for business by reviewing the use of the RPI with a view to changing the calculation to CPI.

9.   Local areas should implement free controlled parking schemes that work for their town centres, and there should be a new parking league table.

10.   Town Teams should focus on making high streets accessible, attractive and safe.

11.   Government should include high street deregulation as part of their ongoing work on freeing up red tape.

12.   Address the restrictive aspects of the 'Use Class' system to make it easier to change the uses of key properties on the high street.

13.   Put betting shops into a separate 'Use Class' of their own.

14.   Make explicit a presumption in favour of town centre development in the wording of the National Planning Policy Framework.

15.   Introduce Secretary of State 'exceptional sign off' for all new out-of-town developments and require all large new developments to have an 'affordable shops' quota.

16.   Large retailers should support and mentor local businesses and independent retailers.

17.   Retailers should report on their support of local high streets in their annual report.

18.   Encourage a contract of care between landlords and their commercial tenants by promoting the leasing code and supporting the use of lease structures other than upward-only rent reviews, especially for small businesses.

19. Explore further disincentives to prevent landlords from leaving units vacant.

20. Banks which own empty property on the high street should either administer these assets well or be required to sell them.

21. Local authorities should make more proactive use of Compulsory Purchase Order powers to encourage the redevelopment of key high street retail space.

22. Empower local authorities to step in when landlords are negligent with new 'Empty Shop Management Orders'.

23. Introduce a public register of high street landlords.

24. Run a high profile campaign to get people involved in Neighbourhood Plans.

25. Promote the inclusion of the High Street in Neighbourhood Plans.

26. Developers should make a financial contribution to ensure that the local community has a strong voice in the planning system.

27. Support imaginative community use of empty properties through Community Right to Buy, Meanwhile Use and a new 'Community Right to Try'.

28. Run a number of High Street Pilots to test proof of concept.

How UK Towns Are Changing to Suit Customer Needs and to be Attractive for Shoppers and Retail Shops

The 12 towns and their plans are:

Bedford – offering mentoring support for high street businesses and community use of empty properties.

Croydon, Greater London – transforming the riot-stricken area's historic Old Town market into a thriving market, food and cultural quarter.

Dartford, Kent – opening up central spaces for use by classes and clubs, from the Scouts to Slimming World and starting a 'school for shopkeepers'.

Bedminster, Bristol – putting Bedminster on the map for street art and street theatre. A bicycle rickshaw service and a review of parking will also tackle the traffic environment.

Liskeard, Cornwall – competing against the edge of town supermarket with a vibrant arts scene, guerrilla gardening and yarn bombing to inject fun back into the town centre.

Margate, Kent – putting education and enjoyment at the heart of the town centre's transformation with courses, 'job club' services and pop-up shops.

Market Rasen, Lincolnshire – drawing customers in by restoring the market town look and feel, advertising free parking and mentoring new businesses.

Nelson, Lancashire – attracting local students with a young persons' cafe, sports activities, and a new art and vintage market.

Newbiggin by the Sea, Northumberland – better branding of the town to draw people in, improving local transport and hosting pop-up shops.

Stockport, Greater Manchester – realising the character and potential of the Markets and Underbanks area with a creative arts complex, outdoor screenings, a new parking strategy and street champions.

Stockton on Tees, North Yorkshire – live entertainment at the Globe Theatre to boost the evening leisure economy alongside specialist high street and evening markets.

Wolverhampton – bringing the city to life with modern-day town criers and on-street performers and a 'dragon's den' style competition to support local entrepreneurs.[1]

1   Harry Wallop, Retail editor, *Daily Telegraph*, 26 May 2012.

Afterword:
Save the Shops – Ten Ways to
Attract Customers

The Internet has brought about a great change in the buying behaviour of customers. The buying moment has shifted from the shop to the couch at home. In the evenings while relaxed at home people search, compare and buy on the Internet. In the coming years buying on the Internet will increase even more, to approximately 35–40% of the non-daily shopping. What's more, the Internet has an influence on the knowledge of the customers. Transparency regarding the products on offer gained by just a quick look on the Internet puts a great deal of pressure on shop prices, and therefore on the profitability of shops. Going to the shops has become a choice, not a necessity.

Shops have of course responded to this. Out-of-town shopping centres have been developed which provide recreational activities, an experience for visitors, restaurants and bars, as well as parking facilities. But this has contributed to the ever increasing number of empty shop premises in the city centres. Longer opening hours was the response to the customers' wish to be able to shop in the evenings and at the weekends, but this has simply led to shopping expenditure being spread out over the available hours rather than to more purchases. All sorts of promotions were introduced, from events to price promotions, from loyalty systems to home deliveries. Competing with the Internet, however, is proving to be very difficult. Shops have to think carefully once again about the customers' future buying behaviour and how to respond to this. Shops remain important to the quality of life of a town. A town without shops is a dead one, and no one wants this. The buying behaviour of customers has dramatically changed and so shops, too, will have to change radically.

Simply changing the existing (shop) model is not sufficient. Not enough would change to attract customers to a shop and entice them into making purchases. Shops have to respond to what the future brings, by integrating technology and responding to the wishes of customers. In addition, shop locations need to be changed; if the customer does not go to the shops, then the shops will have to come to the customer. This will, of course, involve the familiar three-level system: local shops for the daily shopping, high streets and city centres for recreational shopping (social shopping in fun, cosy shops) and social buying in the out-of-town shopping centres for goal-oriented buying. For each cluster a separate strategy will have to be developed in order to attract the customers. Shopping will have to become a conscious choice for customers once again, otherwise shops will disappear for good in many places, with the Internet as the major culprit! Some form of collaboration between the shops found in a particular area is essential. Shops are an important part of a shopping area as much as departments are to a department store.

What Needs to be Done?

The problems that shops face can actually be represented very simply:

$$Profit = turnover\ minus\ costs$$

Due to current developments turnover is declining, whilst the costs are staying more or less the same. This leads to lower profits, and even to losses and bankruptcy. Empty shop premises are on the rise, making shopping areas less attractive and the economic foundation upon which shops are based is eroding. This has to become healthy once more if their future is to be ensured. And it is here where the challenge for the retail sector lies!

1   START A WEBSHOP OR WEBSITE

The first response of the retailer is to also opt for an Internet presence, often in the form of a webshop, in the hope to turn back the tide. The webshop would, however, have to compete with professional Internet providers. This can be very difficult if there is no specific expertise, insufficient budget and if no use is made of all the modern Internet tools such as SEO, SEA, tracking and tracing, and eye tracking. In all cases the Internet would have to be used, but just a website may be sufficient. A website with information about the shop, the collection and contact details such as an email address, physical location, telephone number and a presence on social media. It is important that a potential customer can find the shop when searching on the basis of name or location. A professional webshop is not necessary. A website provides clear information, does not have to be updated so often and is therefore cheaper, too.

In addition to the webshop/website, it is also recommended to be part of a portal such as a product portal, or a portal of the shopping centre or high street, or of a manufacturer. It is also worth considering some form of association with a website that generates a great deal of traffic, such as eBay, Amazon or a price comparison site. This allows you to benefit from the high number of visitors who are already in a buying process. In all cases, the integration between the Internet and the shop is based on the strength of the shop (formula).

2   ENSURE THAT THE SENSES ARE ACTIVATED

However good the Internet may be, only one of the senses (eyes), perhaps a maximum of two (ears), are activated. As a result, shopping on the Internet is always a rational process. Shops therefore have to compete using emotion, by involving other senses. When customers enter a shop, it must be immediately clear that this is not to do with rationality, but with emotion. Rational choices are, for example, a low price, having the right product or being able to order 24/7. Shops will undoubtedly lose out in these areas, but can compensate for this by activating the other senses or feelings. Shops such as Abercrombie & Fitch and Victoria Secret show the importance of the sense of smell. Some studies claim that turnover increases of 15% can be realised by adding a scent to the shop or a department. Music is also important, particularly through audio spots, whereby the music can vary according to the department or product group.

Furthermore, too little is done with lighting. Fluorescent lighting does not give a shop a particularly pleasant or cosy feel. So why not use spot lights and coloured lamps. Ensure that the lighting creates a pleasant ambience. Some products actually do not require a great deal of light (evening clothes, lingerie), so diffuse lighting is ideal for these. Hollister and Abercrombie are perhaps a little extreme in the way they make the entire shop dark and only use spot lights aimed at the products. But the combination of light, scent, design and layout does lead to long queues outside the shops!

Video screens in the shop, possibly combined with 'digital signage', provide an experience and emotion. Videos of manufacturers showing product presentations, fashion shows, music clips or sports matches are usually free and provide an extra dimension in the shop which is not possible on the Internet. Make shopping fun. You don't find any fluorescent lighting in a nightclub; there they clearly do respond to the wishes of the customers.

3   WORK TOGETHER WITH OTHER SHOPS (PORTAL FUNCTION)

Customers often visit a shopping area. Shops therefore have to work together to make the area attractive, so it would therefore make sense if we saw more collaboration here. This can include starting a website or webportal together under joint responsibility, as well as a loyalty system, advertising together and gearing services to one another. By collaborating, the shopping area can become more powerful and costs can be shared. The shop itself would then not have to be found on the Internet. Instead, the shopping area could ensure for a higher positioning on Google and provide direct communication. This would then also stimulate the further support of the shopping public.

4   INTEGRATE LBS AND SOCIAL MEDIA

The application of smartphones in particular offers many opportunities for the retail trade. The smartphone allows you to communicate directly with customers in the shopping centre. A loyalty system that is based on visits, such as shopkicks, rewards customers immediately for their visit to a shopping centre or for their purchases. By integrating smartphones with location-based services, new applications can be provided such as information about shops, shopping routes, special offers and facilities such as childcare, delivery services as well as online direct ordering in the shopping centre. The mobile phone is an identifier, allowing you to recognise and monitor your customers.

5   PROVIDE VIRTUAL CITY WALLS

The Internet does not effectively activate the senses. In the physical world, however, this can be done with sound (audio spots), scents such as a those of a bakery, light through using spot lights, diffuse lighting and colour lighting and, of course, videos on large screens. This experience can be created in the shopping area or shopping centre through virtual city walls. As soon as customers enter, they experience another world of videos, scents, colourful lighting, internet tables, smart mirrors and window displays. There would also be music that is geared towards the shop or department and, of course, services such as delivery services and loyalty services on behalf of the shops or the combined shops.

6 MODIFY THE SHOP CONCEPT, LONG TAIL/SHORT TAIL CONCEPT

The retail sector often refers to the 20/80 rule, whereby 20% of the turnover comes from 80% of the product range, and 80% of the turnover comes from 20% of the product range. Due to the high costs involved in office space rental and the product range, keeping large stocks is no longer cost-effective. One therefore has to look for lower costs for the same or an even higher turnover. This can be achieved by integrating the Internet in the shop using internet tables and smart mirrors.

With the first application it is possible to sell an unlimited product range in the shop which can then be delivered quickly, in the shop or to the home (Internet has no physical limits). The second application enables integration with augmented reality. Here the customer stands in front of a smart mirror, swiping through the collection and seeing immediately how the items of clothing look on them. The items can then be bought at the press of a button.

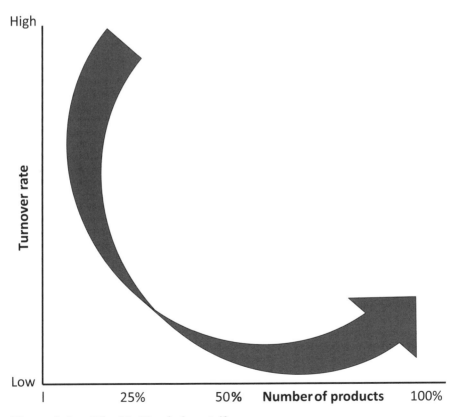

Figure A.1   The 80–20 rule in retail

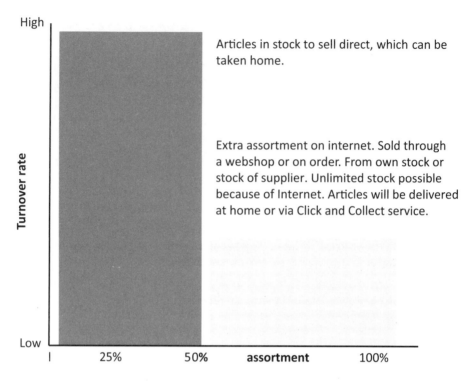

High

Turnover rate

Articles in stock to sell direct, which can be taken home.

Extra assortment on internet. Sold through a webshop or on order. From own stock or stock of supplier. Unlimited stock possible because of Internet. Articles will be delivered at home or via Click and Collect service.

Low

| 25%   50%   assortment   100%

Figure A.2   New retail model based on integration shop/internet

Here, too, the item concerned is often not available in the shop itself (perhaps just a demo item), but can be delivered quickly. Through this integration of Internet applications, a shopkeeper could invest less in the product range and so take fewer risks. What's more, the shop could also be much smaller as it would only have to stock items that had a high turnover. The other items would then be delivered from a different location. It's even recommended to have the manufacturer bear the risk right up to the moment of sale. The manufacturer would then not only take care of the stock control but the delivery as well, allowing the shop to focus mainly on the customers and their wishes! Both the experience and service would increase as a result.

BURBERRY SHOWS THE FUTURE

A space where the digital world meets the physical, the new Burberry store welcomes you to try on clothes in front of a mirror that transforms into a screen. Watch how the piece you're wearing was made and what it looks like in full-flow on the catwalk. Members of staff all have iPads at the ready to help you find exactly what you're looking for and guest

Wi-Fi is available throughout the store – perfect for all you tweeters. Upon entry into the store, a huge screen complete with speakers and stage is there to welcome you. There may even be a live acoustic set, showcasing the best of Britain's new emerging artists. This is the epitome of shopping in style.

Source: Regentstreetonline.com

7   MODIFY THE DISTRIBUTION

The idea that customers come to shops in order to take products away with them is becoming an outdated view. Customers in actual fact come to shops for service, trust, advice and the experience. In the shops they are also able to look at the products. Quite often the customers then go home to buy the products online (showrooming), which is, of course, very frustrating for the shops. Retailers, however, can take advantage of this new buying behaviour by offering these new possibilities to shop. Shops can also collaborate with their suppliers. Stocks no longer have to be kept in the shop, but would need to be delivered quickly, to the shop or the customer's home. This can be achieved by arranging local storage centres with suppliers, enabling quick deliveries to the shop or to the customer who has ordered in the shop or at the webshop online. This helps reduce the costs for the shop (product range investments) and the shop space required (see Burberry example), as well as allows more service to be provided through speedy deliveries to the customer's home. It is also possible to have the local branch deal with the Internet orders instead of having a central Internet stock. By linking the storage system (POS), it can be determined immediately whether the article is in stock at the local shop, after which a speedy delivery can take place. This linking of stocks can be facilitated at branch level as well as by suppliers at sales outlet level after which an allocation of margins takes place. Speedy deliveries, more involvement from the suppliers and local support for customers, whilst the costs for the shops decrease.

8   COMMUNICATION

Communication is key to loyalty. Communicating with customers is therefore very important. This can be done by email but also through the website and smartphones. Smartphones will become increasingly important in the future. By linking Wi-Fi, location-based services and customer recognition, it is possible to respond immediately to the customers' buying behaviour. By using loyalty systems customers can be rewarded for visiting a shop, but they can also activate the app on the telephone. Communicating and monitoring customers now becomes very simple. Not only purchases can be rewarded, but also visits to a shop. By combining a smartphone or tablet with a smart mirror or internet table, a direct connection can be made with the Internet, the webshop and customer data. Smartphones are therefore important during the buying process to help customers to buy (support by cloud services) and during the visit to the shop the customer can be rewarded per product or per activity. Shopkick in America is a good example of this.

9   MODIFY THE BUSINESS MODEL

It is no longer possible for a transaction-oriented business model to be profitable. New components now have to form the basis for the profitability of shops. Service contracts, other agreements with suppliers and a different type of relationship with customers are examples of this. Agreements can be made with suppliers regarding margins, whilst no longer investing in stocks (a type of consignment in the shop or ordering through the Internet in the shop or through the webshop). There should be a strong focus on 'share of wallet': looking at the possible expenditure of each customer and basing the product range (as well as the communication) on this. Retailers can aim for more sales per customer through repeat sales, upsales and cross sales. This involves an expansion of the product range through making agreements with suppliers (drop shipping) and using the possibilities of internet orders: no physical restrictions, so an unlimited product range is possible.

Do not focus on profit (alone), but also at the net promotor score. Do customers wish to recommend your shop or product to others? Customer satisfaction, after all, is the most important weapon in the fight for the customer. Customer satisfaction linked to immediate, regular and targeted communication forms the basis for retailing in the future!

10   RESPOND TO THE BUYING BEHAVIOUR

Why would customers still wish to buy in shops, or in your shop or webshop in particular. There are, of course, the familiar principles of service and hospitality. Keep customers happy and show them that you appreciate their visit and custom. Treat the customer as you would like to be treated yourself, or as you would treat your own friends. There are various techniques available for this, so make use of all of them: social media, webshops, smartphones, smart mirrors, location-based services and Wi-Fi. Listening to the wishes of the customer and responding to the customer behaviour makes the shopkeeper a hunter, not a fisher. And the prey, a satisfied customer!!

Figure A.3   The customer can decide how they will shop

Technology will be the platform for retailing: communication, customer knowledge and services. This will lead to more turnover, less costs (premises) and less costs for stocks (short tail/long tail principle). Retailing can be profitable again.

Index

Note: **Bold** page numbers indicate figures, *italic* numbers indicate tables.